AF632899

HINDU INTERCASTE MARRIAGE IN INDIA
(ANCIENT AND MODERN)

HINDU INTERCASTE MARRIAGE IN INDIA
(ANCIENT AND MODERN)

HARIPADA CHAKRABORTI

Sharada Publishing House
Delhi - 110035
1999

First Published 1999
© Author
All rights reserved. No part of this publication
may be reproduced in any form, or by any means,
without written permission of the author.

ISBN : 81-85616-57-4

SHARADA ₹ 950/-

Published by B.L. Bansal for
SHARADA PUBLISHING HOUSE
40, Anand Nagar, Inderlok, Delhi - 110035
Phones: 5117390, 5116763
Typeset by Neographics
1811 Gyani Bazar, Kotlamubarakpur, New Delhi - 110003
and Printed at Santosh Offset,
Delhi - 110035

Contents

Preface

Here is an humble attempt to draw an outline of the history of Hindu Intercaste Marriage in India, ancient and modern. First I have discussed marriage and its general principles, various forms, polygamy, polyandry and rules of restriction about gotras and pravaras and also intercaste-marriage in early Vedic period.

In the second part, I have tried to trace the history of intercaste marriage and also interracial mixture in ancient India and the gradual evolution of the Hindu society.

The last part contains a detailed discussion of intercaste marriage in modern India along with reform-movement in social sphere and also with legislation in modern India. This treatise ends with views of different scholars and writers of modern India on intercaste marriage and particularly of Rabindranath in the Appendix at the end of this book.

I shall deem my labour amply rewarded if this book is widely read and appreciated and if it helps us to lead a life of love and good will to all so as to bring down an era of peace and harmony in our domestic and social life.

Let me pay my sincere thanks to the Publisher for his keen interest in the publication of this work.

"Ā paritoṣād Viduṣāṃ
na sādhu manye prayoga-Vijñānam".

Naivedya,
P.O. Bolpur (Birbhum)
'Buddha-Pūrṇimā', 1998

HARIPADA CHAKRABORTI

PART - I

CHAPTER I

Marriage in Ancient India

Scholars differ in tracing the history of human marriage. Westermarck in 'History of Human marriage' and Lowie in 'Primitive Society', opine that the earliest form of human organisation was a patriarchal one. The patriarchal family means a group of a man, a woman and their children dominated by the man, formed originally for satisfying the biological need and the need for gathering food. In the primitive period a man or a group of men is supposed to have lived with a man or a group of women. Gradually sex-jealousy and the spirit of individuality, prevailed and prompted a man to contract intimacy and pair-dwelling. The woman also took to a particular man for support and protection, formulating thereby a system of laws and customs which helped the growth of the institution called marriage. It is interesting to note that Darwin,[1] one of the greatest scientists believes in the patriarchal theory.

On the other hand, scholars like McLenan (Primitive marriage), Bechofen (Mother-right) and Brifault (Mothers) have tried to establish the matriarchal theory. According to them, maternal instincts and not the sexual instincts worked behind the formation of the earliest human group consisting of the mother and her children only, the sexual mate playing the part of a stranger. Hence, there was in this stage no concept of husband and wife and as its natural corollary sexual laxity prevailed in the primitive society. Gradually, however, sex-jealousy led to the foundation of marriage system. L. Sternback[2] speaks of the introduction of the system of marriage, first by capture and next, by the purchase of women. Through capture, real or symbolical, a man acquired a slave and in such cases the endogamic system was soon replaced by the exogamic one which became more practical, "because through the union of two tribes a more powerful combination was effected", which "assisted the tribe in protecting itself against its enemies". The form of marriage by purchase is still existing among races of a lower stage of civilisation. According to this form, the girl under the guardianship of her father or guardian was treated as merchandise which could be sold for the highest price to any man. The girl had no choice of her husband and she was practically nothing more than a slave of her husband. It is more likely that a woman in the primitive period felt the need of protection of both herself and her new-born child in the period of her confinement and hence she chose her permanent companion in life. R.B. Pandey[3] remarks: "It appears that marriage has its source in the family, rather than family in marriage and the very roots of the permanent union of the sexes are found in the parental duties".

Whatever may be accepted as the origin of marriage, promiscuity was replaced by the system of marriage which proved to be efficient device to regulate the instinct of sex which is by far the dominant feature of all animals, not excepting even man. Man is no doubt a rational animal and he has by virtue of reason evolved one of the earliest institutions like marriage and thereby enriched the society by the formulation of ethical codes.

In ancient India as elsewhere, people were mainly nomadic. Hunting and cattle-rearing formed the chief means of their occupation. The Ṛgveda speaks of lifting of cattle as one of the reasons of war. Gradually, the society took to agriculture. To some Rāma, the hero of the Rāmāyaṇa symbolises the spirit of expansion of agriculture; Sītā, (furrow-mark), an embodiment of agriculture was kidnapped and it was not an isolated event. The introduction of agriculture transformed the society. Gradually the life of villages and towns, governed by the kings had emerged.

India turned her attention to make the life in home sweeter by the cultivation of the spirit of sacrifice which is best reflected in the Rāmāyaṇa. Home was accepted as a place not merely for the enjoyment of material pleasures of life but also as a stepping stone for the sublimation of one's life by the proper discharge of ethico-religious duties by the members of a family. That is why the sages of India stressed upon the importance of household life which enlivened the different other limbs of the society. Each householder was duty-bound to perform certain social obligations, as reflected later on in the concept of the 'pañca-mahāyajña'.

The Aryans, while they infiltrated into the soil of the Saptasindhu region, had to live with the pre-Aryan people of heterogenous elements and to face their customs. Gradually there sprang forth a new composite culture, born of the fusion of various elements. Each community tried to preserve its purity and marriage, being the root of household life, each tried to maintain the integrity of its own culture through the observance of some distinct customs and traditions. Hence, we can naturally expect that marriage was not treated as a mere personal matter but as a social institution. Personal desires had to be some times curtailed in the interests of the society as an organic whole. Of course, love-marriage where personal interests prevailed was not wanting even as early as the Ṛgvedic period. The Aryans had to adjust with the changed circumstances when they penetrated further into different parts of India and they had to approve of different forms of marriage in which instinctive desires were the main factors and which were naturally looked down upon by the later jurists as undesirable (*adharmya*) marriages.

It is interesting to note that the ancient Indian society evolved in course of centuries the system of varṇāśrama-dharma, i.e. the laws regulating different castes and stages of life. The householder's life was, after all, a means to the highest end of attaining emancipation and so, homa being the centre of activities for one's upward journey to the realisation of one's true self, marriage was naturally evolved to regulate man's sex-life and to maintain balance and harmony in the life of both man and woman according to the ethical principles of life, better known as 'dharma', as reflected in the terms like sahadharmiṇī and ardhāṅginī.

It has been noted above that marriage in the primitive society here, as elsewhere sometime merely meant a sex-life between a group of men and of women and their off- springs were regarded as belonging to the group. R.S. Sharma draws our attention to some traces of promiscuity in ancient Indian society in an article, read and published in Indian History Congress (1967). Meyer "opines that there is nothing of promiscuity in Vedic literature". But we know of the myth of Prajāpati being enamoured of his daughter. Puṣan wooed his mother. The *Aitareya Brāhmaṇa* refers in a gāthā to the fact that for the sake of sons even a mother or a sister was accepted as a wife. Manu was begotten by Brahmā on his daughter Śatarūpā. So it may not be unlikely that these cases remind us of the practice of the primitive patriarchal society where sons were of greater need in day to day life. There are traces of promiscuity also in the *Mahābhārata*. The women of the Madra country and specially of Balhika are mentioned in the Karṇaparvan as licentious and indulging in sexual intercourse in the open. The *Rājataraṅginī*[5] states that the Brāhmaṇas of Gandhāra lived in incest, obviously echoing the tradition of this part of India persisting from hoary antiquity. The *Mahābhārata*[6] also refers to the story of Uddālaka and Śvetaketu. Śvetaketu's mother was snatched by a Brāhmaṇa in the presence of his father. But his father told him that there was nothing in it to get furious, because all the women in this world were uncovered and self-willed. But Śvetaketu would not accept this and he established the rule that the wife who neglects her husband and the husband who violates the unmarried girl shall be guilty of killing the embryo. The gāthā in the *Āpas. Dh. S.*[7] and *Bodn. Dh. S.*[8] speaks of the time when little value was placed on the conjugal faith of a woman. Sons like 'gūḍhotpannā', noted in the Smṛtis seem to be reminiscent of the promiscuous relations of the earlier days.

As an instance of group marriage we may cite the case of Draupadī from the *Mahābhārata*. Yudhiṣṭhira says that they followed the path trodden by succession of ancestors and that their mother had enjoined it. He gives the instances of Jaṭilā, daughter of Gotama and of Vārkṣī, daughter of a sage, both equally virtuous women, who were the wives of seven and ten husbands respectively. However, this practice of polyandry was not in use in the period of composition or revision of the

Mahābhārata, because special divine authority was required to justify its occurrence among the respectable persons conceiveable even in earlier ages.[9]

However, with the advancement of society the collective marriage was replaced by individual marriage which may be traced in the earliest phase when the bride was forcibly lifted from her parents, better known as marriage by capture, already referred to. Mc Lenan[10] suggests that marriage by force took place all over the world in the earliest phase, but with the rise of the concept of individualism and private ownership individual marriage system came into practice and the concept of exogamy, i.e. marriage with the member of the external clan appeared with full vigour, as reflected in the system of a-sagotra-marriage. Gradually at a certain stage the patriarchal family came to be accepted as an ideal and women took to the life of chastity. Thus the system of marriage grew up as an institution of the civilised society, with equal importance attached to both the progeny and the ancestors.

REFERENCES

1. *Descent of Man*, II, p. 36.
2. *Ann. of the Bhandarkar Or. Res. Inst.*, Vol. XXII, 1941, p. 202.
3. *Hindu Saṃskāras*, Banaras, 1949, p. 268.
4. Jolly, *Hindu Law and Custom*, p. 106 fn. 2.
5. 1. 308.
6. (Kumbha, ed.), 128-9.15.
7. II, 13.7.
8. II, 3.34.
9. Cf. *Ind. Ant.* (Sept. 1877), p. 262; Reprinted, Indological Book Reprint Corporation (Delhi, 1971).
10. *Studies in Anc. History*, p. 9.

CHAPTER II

Intercaste Marriage in Early Vedic Period

Let us enquire into the system of intercaste marriage or rather the inter-racial marriage in the early Vedic period. It is interesting to note that in the earliest stratum of the Vedic society there was little caste-system among the Vedic Aryans. A.C. Das[1] says: "The Vedic Aryans were divided into classes and not castes and each class was named after the work it had to perform". We come across different occupations of different members of the same family in the Ṛc. (ix. 112). From the close scrutiny of some other ṛcs[2] we may conclude that one could follow any occupation according to one's own aptitude or likes. We come across fresh, two varṇas, Ārya and Dāsa, obviously on the basis of colour or race-distinction; then three varṇas, Brāhmaṇa, Kṣattriya and Vaiśya; and last, four including the Śūdras, as found in the Puruṣa-sūkta.[3]

According to D.R. Bhandarkar[4] the term Śūdra denoted originally a foreigner or a non-aryan: - "There can be no doubt that śūdras denoted foreigners or aboriginals who were different from Āryas in stock or religion". In the *Atharvaveda*[5] we find mention of the contrast between the āryas and the śūdras. Müir[6] thinks that the principle of division of labour was established in the Vedic society when the Vedic Aryans had increased their number, while "gradually increasing number of the adjoining barbarians is becoming incorporated in the growing society as slaves or handicraftsmen of the lowest description". Max Müller says,[7] "There is no authority whatsoever in the hymns of the Veda for the complicated system of caste, no authority for the degraded position of the śūdras. There is no law to prohibit the different classes of the people from living together, from eating and drinking together, no law to prohibit the marriage of people belonging to different castes". V. M. Apte[8] also remarks in the same strain: "The heredity of occupations was therefore not yet a recognised principle, far less an established fact. Of the other essential features of the caste system, i.e. prohibition of interdining and inter-marriage, no such restriction is even remotely hinted at in the hymns of the Ṛgveda".

Intercaste marriages, both anuloma and pratiloma were in practice in the Ṛgvedic period, as evidenced by the ṛc (I.126) reporting that Kakṣivān, the Ṛṣi married the grand-daughter of King Bhavya and by another ṛc (I.112-19) refering to the marriage of Vimada, a Brahmin with a Rājanya princess, daughter of Purumitra. Similarly the ṛc (VIII. 1.34) speaks of Śāśvatī, daughter of Ṛṣi Aṅgiras being married to king Āsaṅga. Wooing or love-making was not unknown to Vedic Aryans and some times, if the parents put any objection to the union of such couple, two lovers eloped to an unknown place and extracted consent from the parents of the daughter. Thus, when women were not held in seclusion and when they could choose their own partners, it is not unlikely that intercaste marriages were more frequent in the society. The case of Śvāvāśya, son of a priest may be cited here to show how he ardently loved a princess and also was loved by her but the queen mother stopped this marriage by her veto.

Not only intercaste but also inter-racial union took place in the Vedic and post-Vedic period. S.K. Chatterjee[9] says that "all non-aryans within the framework of Aryan-dominated society, ... were at first given the general name of śūdras". This happened when the Aryans conquered many non-aryan territories and these śūdras were relegated to an inferior status, with considerable disabilities. The epics also record the fights between the Aryans and non-aryan peoples. Slater in his "Dravidian element in Indian culture" speaks of these stages of such inter-racial conflict. At the first stage the non-aryans were killed and their cities and wealth were devastated. The second stage marks the wholesale slavery of the conquered peoples and the last stage shows both fighting and alliance with the non-aryans. thus the period of gradual fusion of culture by mutual intercourse. Thus this period witnessed the innumerable cases - of intermarriage between two different races and the Great epic bears such evidences as the marriage of Śāntanu with Satyavatī, daughter of a fisherman, of Bhīma with the Rākṣasa princess Hiḍimbā, of Arjuna with the Nāga princess Ulūpī and of Abhimanyu with Uttarā, daughter of the non-aryan King Virāṭa.

The role of 'dharma' in Indian marriage was distinctly manifested when sacrifice began to be the sole religion of the Vedic Aryans. The *Śatāpatha Brāhmaṇa*[10] asserts that "wife is the half of one's own self. (*ardhohavā eṣoātmano Yajjāyā tasmāt yāvat jāyāṃ na vindate naiva tāvat prajāyate asarvo hi tāvad bhavati*). So long as one does not have a wife, one does not beget a son one is not complete. The same idea is also expressed in the *Tait. Saṃ.*[11] and *Ait. Brāhmaṇa.*[12] Wife is regarded as one's ardhāṅginī not only from the biological point of view but also from the religious standpoint. The husband and wife have to adjust themselves for mutual interests even at the expense of one's own and as a result the virtue of fidelity is naturally cultivated by each of them. Chastity of woman was praised equally as that of man, as reflected in the lines of a later jurist[13] *-sva-dāranirata-ś-ca smṛtaḥ*. The conjugal relation was believed to be persisting not only in this life but also in after life. The wife was called 'jāyā', because the husband believed himself to be born in her as the son and the Ṛv.[14] speaks of the prayer: "May I obtain immortality through progeny (*prajābhi-r-agne-amṛtatvam-aśyām*). Sons play an important part in the cult of ancestor-worship. This position of wife and son led to the formulation of ethics and marriage was held as an institution in which the family-tie became more enriched with the silken relationship of wife and children.

The wife was indispensable in one's discharge of religious duties, i.e. in the performance of sacrifices and other duties and so was called sahadharmiṇī. As early as the Ṛgveda[15] the Indo-Aryans "worshipped the fire who is worthy of worship". Later on in the period of the Brāhmaṇas[16] when firecult reached its acme in the shape of sacrifices, the husband and wife performed sacrifices jointly with the prayer 'May they be of one mind and destroy their foes, (*saṃjānānau vijahatam arātiḥ*). Thus marriage was closely associated with the religious fervour and was sanctified in the shape of a sacrament. Pāṇini[17] also refers to a wife as 'patnī', because she was a partner in the performance of a sacrifice.

Thus marriage came to be recognised in the Aryan society not simply as a sex-alliance but as a sacrament, practically for the fulfilment of ethical and spiritual aspirations of life. It was and is still accepted as a means of sublimation of one's baser instincts to the higher level of divine life and so as a refined state of sacrament or saṃskāra.

In the early Vedic period when free marriage was the fashion of the day, the ceremony of marriage consisted in only holding the hand of the bride before the sacrificial fire (pāṇigrahaṇa), but later in the sūtra period which witnessed the rise of the concept of marriage as sacrament, the ceremony took the form of a religious rite like that of homa and saptapadīgamana (going seven steps) which alone made the marriage legal according to jurists like Manu.[18]

"*pāṇigrahaṇikā mantrā niyataṃ dāralakṣaṇam/teṣāṃ niṣṭhā tu vijñeyā vidvadbhiḥ saptame pade//* Of course, the śūdra who had no access to the performance of sacrifices by means of Vedic martras, were allowed to marry only by the holding of the bridegroom's garment by the bride. (*śūdrasya tu tat daśāgrahaṇam amantrakam*).[19]

It is interesting to point out the remark of P.V. Kane[20] on marriage: "The purpose of marriage, according to Ṛgveda, was to enable a man, by becoming a householder to perform sacrifices to the gods and to procreate sons". This Vedic ideal was however, accepted by both the schools of Dharma and Artha but differing in one point. The Dharmaśāstras regard marriage as a sacrament, while the Arthaśāstra-writers think of it as a contract. Hence, according to Dharma school marriage is an indissoluble tie and so divorce was rarely allowed only in special circumstances; but

Kauṭilya made the rules of divorce more liberal. K.P. Jayaswal observes: "The Dharma Schools, it should be remembered, regarded marriage as a sacrament. But the Artha regarded it as a contract whether entered into by parties themselves or vicariously through guardians. The consequences which flowed from the contract view find expression in the Artha laws. There could be a forced dissolution by the State. There is a great opposition offered on the point in our Dharma codes". Manu[21] says: "Let mutual fidelity continue upto death", This may be regarded as the summary of the highest law for husband and wife. But Yājñavalkya, a renowned jurist of the Dharma school, possibly of the Gupta period, who[22] ordains:

> *"Sakṛt pradīyate kanyā haraṃ-s-tām caura-daṇḍabhāk/*
> *dattām-api haret pūrvā-cchreyāṃ-ś-ced vara āvrajet//*
>
> - is again found to speak nothing against the punarbhū *(punarbhūḥ saṃskṛtā punaḥ)*.[23]

Bye the bye, it may be pointed out that the Atharvaveda[24] (*Yā purvaṃ patiṃ vitvāthānyāṃ vindate param/pañcaudanaṃ ca tāvajam dadāto na vi yaṣataḥ//*) declares that a Punarbhū or a twice-married woman shall not be separated from her second husband but shall go to the same heaven (samānaloka) with him, if they present a goat with five rice-dishes. According to M. Barth, "the more rigid provisions represent rather the ideals of strict and exclusive Brāhmaṇas than the current practice of the ages when they lived. The expression- *'dattām-api haret pūrvāt'* of Yāj., may be taken to mean that he is in favour of divorce, if the groom is not upto the expectation and if the better suitor is available. Though Vijñāneśwara or Bālambhaṭṭa interprets this verse in the light of Dharma code that this taking back of the bride is possible only when the marriage-ceremony is still incomplete before the seventh step of the bride, it is difficult to read the mind of Yāj., specially when he allows a punarbhū and it may not be unlikely that though belonging to the Dharma school, Yāj. was influenced by the Artha school to regard marriage not only as a sacrament but also as a contract.

REFERENCES

1. *Ṛgvedic Culture,* p. 128.
2. V. 23.1., VI, 31.1 and X 39.14.
3. Rv. X. 90.
4. *Some aspects of Anc. Ind. Culture,* p. 10.
5. XIX, 62.1.
6. *Original Sanskrit Texts,* V, p. 452.
7. Vol. II, p. 311.
8. *The Vedic Age,* p. 388.
9. *Indo-Asia Culture,* July 1954.
10. V. 2, 1, 10.
11. VI. 1, 8, 5.
12. 1,2, 4-5.
13. *Yaj.* 1.8.
14. V. 4.10.
15. 1.72.5.
16. *Tait. Brah.,* III, 7.5.52.
17. IV. 1.33 - *'patyu-r-na-Yajña-saṃyyoge.*
18. VIII. p. 227.
19. *Gṛhastha-ratnākara,* p. 57.
20. *H.D.S.,* II, i, p. 428.
21. IX. 101-2.
22. 1.65.
23. *Yāj.* 1.67.
24. IX. 5.27.

CHAPTER III

Forms of Marriage

Now let us discuss the various forms of marriage, as noted in the Dharma literature. Manu[1] speaks of eight forms, as follows:

> *"brāhmo daiva-s-tathaivārṣaḥ prājāpatya-s-tathāsuraḥ/*
> *gāndharvo rākṣasa-ś-caiva paiśāca-s-cāṣṭamo'dhamaḥ.//*

The *Mānava Gṛhyasūtra*, however, mentions only two forms, brāhma and śaulka (i.e. āsura). *Āpastamba* speaks of only six of the above list excepting prājāpatya or kāya form, second in the list. Yāj. follows Manu's list with the exception that he mentions kāya inplace of prājāpatya and that he speaks of paiśāca as one by deception.

Manu[2] defines brāhma marriage as "the gift of a daughter, after decking her with valuable garments and honouring her (with jewels) to a man learned in the Vedas and of good conduct, when the father himself invites". (tr. by Kane): *"ācchādya cārcayitvā ca śruta-śīlavate svayaṃ/āhūya dānaṃ kanyāyābrāhmo dharmaḥ prakīrtitaḥ//.*" This form may be traced even in the Ṛgveda as in the case of the marriage of Sūryā with Soma. He[3] speaks of the daiva form (*Yajñe tu vitate samyagṛtvije karma-kurvate/alamkṛtya sutādānaṃ daivaṃ dharmaṃ pracakṣate//*) as one "When the father gives away his daughter after decking her (with ornaments) to a priest who duly officiates at a sacrifice during the course of its performance. In the ārṣa form[4] we hear of "a gift of one's daughter after taking one pair of cattle (a cow and a bull) or two pairs only as a matter of fulfilling the law (and not as a sale of the girl): *ekaṃ go-mithunaṃ dvevā varādādāya dharmataḥ/Kanyāpradānaṃ vidhivadārṣo dharmaḥ sa ucyate//*". The prājāpatya marriage is also defined as "the gift of a daughter after the father has addressed the couple with the words - "may both of you perform your religious duties together" and after he has honoured the bridegroom (with madhuparka): "*Sahobhau caratāṃ dharmam iti vācā' nubhāṣya ca/ kanyāpradānam abhyarcya prājāpatyo vidhiḥ smṛtaḥ//*".[5] In the āsura form Manu[6] says: *Jñātibhyo draviṇaṃ datva kanyāyai caiva śaktitaḥ/ kanyā-pradānam svācchandyād āsuro dharma ucyate-//*. i.e. the girl is given away at the father's will after the bridegroom gives as much wealth as he can afford to pay to the relatives of the girl. The union of a girl and the bridegroom by their mutual consent is known as gāndharva,[7] which springs from the passion of love and as intercourse as its purpose, (*icchayānyonya-saṃyogaḥ kanyāyāśca varasya ca/ gāndharvaḥ sa tu vijñeyo maithunyaḥ kāmasambhavaḥ//*). Manu[8] speaks of the rākṣasa form as the forcible abduction of a maiden from her house, while she weeps and cries aloud after her kinsmen have been slain, wounded and their homes are broken open. (*hatvā cchittvā ca bhittvā ca krośantīṃ rudatīṃ gṛhāt/ prasahya kanyāharaṇam rākṣaso vidhirucyate//*). In this form the bridegroom did not wait for the consent of the father of the girl or of the girl herself, but he took her off by force. The definition given by Manu is noted above. Viṣṇu (*Yuddhaharaṇena rākṣasaḥ*) and Yāj. (*rāksaso Yuddhaharaṇāditi*) show that this method was originally in practice among the early warring tribes. Sometimes the lovers came into clash with their guardians and the bridegroom had to capture and elope the bride as in the epic instances of Rukmiṇī and Subhadrā and even in the earlier Vedic cases of Vimada and Purumitra. Bhīṣma is said to have called the rākṣasa process as the best for the kṣattriyas in the Mahābhārata:[9] *Kṣattriyānāṃ tu vīryena praśastaṃ haraṇaṃ balāt*. Last, "when a man has intercourse with a girl stealthily, while she is asleep or intoxicated or disordered in mind (or unconscious), that is, according to Manu,[10] the paiśāca form which is the most sinful of all forms". (*Suptāṃ mattāṃ pramattāṃ vā raho yatropagacchati/ sa pāpiṣṭho vivāhānāṃ paiśācaḥ prathito' dhamaḥ"//*).

Brāhma indicates its association with Brahman (the Veda) and it reminds us of Brahmā, the creator of the entire universe or

Svayambhū. Hence this form stands first in the list of Manu, obviously for the reason that it was sanctioned by the Vedas and that it reminds us of the Hindu ideal of marriage in which the husband is born anew in his wife. The name daiva is indicative of the gift of a girl to a brāhmaṇa who is a god on earth (bhūdeva) and who is associated with the sacrifice. Thus, it is nothing but a sacrificial gift. Ārṣa is also a gift of the girl according to injunctions (vidhivat), of course after taking a pair of cows (or a cow and a bull) as a matter of Dharma (dharmataḥ). It is hardly acceptable that 'this practice was prevalent probably among the Ṛṣi-s as K.N. Chatterjee[11] would have us believe it, simply because the word ārṣa is derived from Ṛṣi. Keith finds in it a trace of purchase in a valid form. Manu[12] himself mentions its character as a sale (of the daughter): *ārṣe go-mithunaṃ śulkam kecid āhur mṛṣaiva tat/ alpo'pyevaṃ mahān vāpi vikraya-s tāvadeva saḥ//*. But still this form is more commendable than the rest as reflected in the use of the terms vidhivat and dharmataḥ in connection with Kanyā-pradānaṃ and as it has been associated with brāhma, daiva and prājāpatya to form the group of four forms, treated as commendable for the brāhmaṇas. (*Caturo brāhmaṇasyādyān praśastān kavayo viduḥ*).[13] Kauṭilya's note of distinction between the two groups is clearer on the present issue, "the first four (brāhma, prājāpatya, ārṣa and daiva) are ancestral customs of old and are valid for their being approved by the father. (*Pitṛ-pramāṇāś catvāraḥ pūrve dharmyāḥ*), while the rest are to be sanctioned by both the father and the mother, for it is they that receive the money (śulka) paid by the bridegroom for their daughter". (*mātā-pitṛpramāṇāḥ śeṣāḥ tau hi śulkaharau duhituḥ*).

Prājāpatya is derived from Prajāpati and it is not unlikely that in this form the groom who is a suitor, as distinctly mentioned by Yāj.[14] (*Yā dīyate arthine*) is desired to lead the life of a householder by the performance of religious rites in co-operation with his partner (*sahobhau caratāṃ dharmam*). Herein we find the rise of the concept of children and of joint performance of 'dharma' as the end of marriage. Medhātithi, while commenting on Manu (III, 30) says that it is a case of contract that the suitor would never leave the bride in matters of dharma, artha and kāma (*Yadyenām māticarasi dharmārtha-kāmeṣu tadā tulyam iyam dīyate iti kṛtasaṃvitkāyām* .....), that is, he should ever remain a householder so long as the bride is living and Medhātithi observes that this form is inferior to Brāhma only for this element of contract (*anayaiva saṃvidā doṣenāsya nyūnatā* ....). However, in both Brāhma and Prājāpatya forms we find a free gift of the girl by her father and the fulfilment of the sense of sacrament.

Next Āsura. Derived from asura it conveys the idea of what is malevolent. It is a clear case of the sale of the girl. Only for this commercial character it had been denounced in the society and Vasiṣṭha speaks of it as mānuṣa, showing thereby the utilitarian consideration of common men. The *Bodh. D.S.*[15] however, speaks of āsura and rākṣasa marriages to be valid for kṣattriyas. (*Kṣattradharmānugatau*) and he opines that the vaiśyas and śūdras are without any restriction in taking their wives (*ayantritakalatrā hi vaiśya-śūdrā bhavanti*), showing thereby the mutual merging of these two castes. However, there is no doubt that in the āsura form the bridegroom had to pay money to the relatives and to the bride. It is well-known to us that the classical Greek writers[16] mention the sale of young girls in open markets in N.W. India and people purchased them to make wives. Bodhāyana[17] and Manu[18] denounce this sort of sale of girls. It is interesting to note that though daiva and āsura fall under the same category of sale of girls, of course, in a veiled form, they were approved by the jurists, because we have already noticed that these two were associated with sacrifices and because these were in practice among the śiṣṭas. Custom had the force of law and this custom is also referred to by Megasthenes.[19] The āsura form is also referred to in the *Ṛgveda*[20] (*aśravaṃ hi bhūridāvattarā Vāṃ Vijāmāturuta dhāvāśyālāt*) and also in the *Nirukta*[21] (*aśrauṣam hi bahudātṛtarau vāṃ vijāmātur asusamāptājjāmātuḥ/ vijamāte iti śaśvad dākṣiṇājaḥ krītāpatim ācakṣate/ a-su-samāpta iva varo'abhipretaḥ*"). Daṇḍin refers to this form of marriage contracted by merchants and lower classes in *ASK*[22] and *DKC.*[23]

Gāndharva is again derived from Gandharva who is known as libidinous. (*Strī-Kāmāvai Gandharvāḥ* in T.S. vi, 1, 6, 5). This form of marriage is heard of in the *Ṛgveda.*[24] (*Kiyatī yoṣā maryato vadhūyoḥ pariprītā paṇyasā vāryaṇa/bhadrā .... Vanute jane cit//*). It must have been very favourite with the Kṣattiryas, as referred to in the *Mahābhārata* and also in Kālidāsa's *Abhijñānaśakuntalam*. This is a union effected without the consent of the father or guardian, depending only on mutual consent. According to *Bodhāyana D.S.*,[25] however it was valid for the Vaiśyas, though he says that it was valid for all, according to some, on account of love being its main factor. (*Gāndharvamapyeke praśaṅsanti sarveṣāṃ snehānugatatvāt*). The gāndharva form may be older from the historical point of view but it wás not approved by the Dharmaśāstras possibly for the reason that marriage was looked upon as a social institution and as a means of sublimation of passions and desires. Passions and desires playing more prominent part in such love-marriages, this form was denounced, as reflected in *Abhijñānaśakuntalam*[26] of Kālidāsa. In *Raghuvaṃśam*[27] (*śrīḥ sābhilaṣāpi guroranujñāṃ dhīreva Kanyā pitur ācakāṃkṣa*) also Kālidāsa praises a discreet daughter waiting for the consent of her father in the matter of marriage, instead of rushing to marry out of her own freewill. The Dharma school never entertains the ideal of women's liberty and so this form is naturally expected to be disapproved by this school.

The Saṅgam literature[28] preserves the reminiscences of the age when the only form of marriage was the system of the Yalors or Gandharvas who played on Yal (Vīṇā). Vātsyāyana[29] refers to this system as the best of marital relations. Daṇḍin[30] refers to the Gāndharva form as befitting the Kṣattriyas, mentioned in connection with courtesans, married by men of even the higher classes.

Two other forms of marriage, effected without the consent of the father or guardian are Rākṣasa and Paiśāca, equally denounced by the Dharma school. Manu[31] says distinctly that "from the remaining four blameable marriages spring sons who are cruel and speakers of untruth, who hate the Veda and sacred law". The Rākṣasa marriage was resorted to by the Kṣattriyas and it was known as 'kṣattra' to some Dharmaśāstra-writers.

Arjuna married Subhadrā by this form. In the historical period Pṛthvīrāj took to this method to win Saṃyuktā. This form was used in some shape by some of the Proto-Austroloid tribes like the Gonds and the Birhols still to-day. Hence we may infer that marriage by capture was in vogue from very early times till it was sanctioned, though denounced, by the later Dharma School. Āpastamba and Vasiṣṭha are quite silent about these two. Dionyssus speaks of such marriage practised in ancient Greece. Westermarck[32] opines that "marriage by capture has been succeeded by marriage by purchase". Paiśāca has been derived from piśāca and it is associated with the activities of the Piśācas who are supposed to act stealthily at night. Manu's[34] attitude towards this form has already been pointed out: "the most heinous and worst of all" and he has assigned it to the Śūdras. Āpastamba does not accept it as marriage and he is silent about it. Yāj.[34] also counts it as a marriage by deception (*paiśācaḥ kanyākāchalāt*). Indeed rape cannot be legalised in any cultured society. Kauṭilya[35] (*sarveṣāṃ prītyāropaṇam apratiṣiddham*), however, legalises it by the later consent of the guardians, of course, thinking of the helpless condition of the distressed girl who, otherwise, had no prospect of marriage. Even today the law courts are resorted to for putting pressure for marriage in such cases of fraud or violence.

The Svayaṁvara, mentioned in the epics, Dharmaśāstras and in classical literature reminds us of the Gāndharva form in another shape. Thus we have here a clear picture of different forms of marriage in ancient India and it is interesting to note that marriage by all forms must be taken to be complete, when homa and saptapadi-gamana are performed, thus obviously solemnised with a religious tinge. The ṛc[36] (*svayaṃ sā mitraṃ vanute jane cit*), refers distinctly to the self choice of husbands by maidens. Sāyaṇa finds in this ṛc the earliest instance of the svayaṁvara ceremony (*svayaṁvara-dharmeṇa prārthayate*), followed later on by Draupadī, Damayantī and other maidens choosing Arjuna, Ṅala and others. (*Draupadī-Damayantyādikā vadhūḥ ..... svayam-eva mitraṇ priyam Arjuna-Nalādikaṃ patim vanute yācate*). This conventional system of Svayaṁvara is referred to in the history as late as the 11th cent. A.D. The Dvyāśraya-mahākāvya of Hemachandra[37] mentions a svayaṁvara in which Mahendra of Nāḍol (*c.* 1000 A.D.) held this function for his sisters, Durlabhadevī and Lakṣhmī. Pṛthvīrājavijaya[38] of Jayānaka refers to Kalāvatī being married with the ruler of Kāṇyakubja, most probably Bhoja (836-888 A.D.). Bilhana also describes the svayaṁvara of Candralekhā, daughter of the Śilāhāra prince of Karahāṭa (mod. Karad) choosing Āhavamalla or Vikramāṅka, the Cālukya king of Kalyāṇa of the latter half of the 11th cent. A.D. (*Vikramāṅka-deva-carita*, canto IX). From the *Kādambarī* also (Pūrvabhāga, para 225) we learn of this system, allowed in the Dharmaśāstras from the mouth of Patralekhā (*Yaḥ svayaṃ vṛtavatyaḥ patīn*).

Next about polyandry. It was a common practice among the people of ancient Bactria, Sogdiana and China and among the ancient Medes[39] and also among the ancient Greeks.[40] It is interesting to note that collective marriage was in practice in the Indo-Iranian stage or even earlier. Polyandry prevailed even among the Vedic Aryans, as reflected in the myth[41] of Sūryā marrying twin brothers, Aświns. The term sādhāraṇī in the ṛc[42] (*parā śubhrā ayāso yavyā sādhāraṇyeva maruto mimikṣuḥ*) indicates the prevalence of this system, as Maruts are heard of as interested in their common young wife. The use of the term Varā (husbands) in the plural in the *AV.*[43] (*ātmanvatyur-varā nārīyam - āgan tasyāṃ naro vapata vījamasyāṃ*) and of patibhyo in *Pāraskara-Gṛhya-sūtra*[44] (*sā naḥ patibhyo jāyaṃ dāgne prajayā saha*) meaning "Mayst thau give back, Agni, to the husbands the wife along with offspring", and also the use of devṛkāmā in the *AV.*[45] confirm our issue. Fraternal polyandry allowed a family of brothers to marry a family of sisters, as reflected in the hymn of the *AV.*[46] (*jāminiccha pitṛ-ṣadaṃ nyaktāṃ sa te bhāgo januṣā tasya viddhi*). meaning "O Viśvāvasu, seek thou a sister sitting among the Fathers, inserted; that is thy portion by right of birth, know thou that". The existence of this system is also expressed in a clear-cut way in the argument of Yudhiṣṭhira,[47] (*pūrveṣāṃ ā nupūrvyeṇā yātam vartmānuyāmahe*), when the king Drupada and his son Dhṛṣṭadyumna put objection to Draupadi's marriage with five Pāṇḍavas. The system of levirate (niyoga) in which the younger brother known as devara (secondary husband) had the prior claim is also reminiscent of the practice of polyandry in our ancient society. The offer of a bride to a family (Kula) and not to a particular individual, as referred to in *Āpas. D.S.*[48] and in Bṛhaspati's Dh. S., as quoted in *Smṛti-Chandrīkā*[49] is also a clear indication of the system. Alberuni referred to its existence among the hill tribes "Stretching from the region of Panchir into the neighbourhood of Kashmir" among whom it is still prevalent".[50] Col. Wilks notes that among Polygars of Totier caste in South India several brothers in one family shared one wife. Polyandry was discouraged even at the time of the *Ait. Brāhmaṇa* which shows that a man could have many wives but a woman could have only one husband; and the *Mbh.* (1.160.36) reiterates the same tradition. The Bṛhad-devatā comments on the Ṛgvedic passage- "With this verse the wife ascends (the pyre of) the dead. The younger brother of the deceased, having recited (this verse) prevents her". The brother-in-law does not claim his right over her.

Polyandry exists to-day in some areas of Dehradun district and in Rawain and Jaunsar (dist. Dehradun) of the former Tehri state. Among the Khasas Levirate (instead of polyandry) is in practice. But a woman was considered to be the joint property of all brothers, though the eldest had the conjugal right so long as he was present in the house. His absence however, provided them with ample opportunities.

"The Khasas are known to have, along with polyandry, monogamy and even polygamy as prevalent forms of marital union". (Marriage and Family in India by K.M. Kapadia, p. 71, Cal. 1968). Mr. Kapadia suggests that "polyandry is some times due to a high bride-price".

Non-fraternal polyandry is another form in which one woman has many husbands with whom she cohabits in turn and these husbands may not be brothers. In case of a birth of a child any one of the husbands is accepted as its social parent by a particular ritual. The causes of these forms of polyandry are said to be

(i) lesser number of women, (ii) poverty, (iii) bride-price, (iv) backwardness in respect of culture and also strengthening of joint-family.

Polyandry even of non-fraternal type seems to have existed also among the Nairs. The Malabar Marriage Commission speaks of its prevalence in Ponnami and Waluvanad taluks. Panikkar says: "Marriage of cross-cousins being the orthodox form of marriage, all brothers are potential husbands of a woman and hence after her marriage with any of them all the brothers treat her "half as a sister and half as a wife". Nair marriage is generally called 'sambandham'. Any girl of Nairs could have such relation not only with a male of her own caste or of a upper caste but also with a Brahmin or Kṣattriya. Alliance with a Nambudri family is recognised as an honour. But sambandham, though legal was not always permanent. Marriage among the Nairs was stabilised by the Malabar Marriage Act of 1896, which took Sambandham to be legalised by registration. Hence until recently polyandry seems to have been in practice among the tribe of Nairs who were once matrilineal.

Polyandry[51] seems to have existed also among the patrilineal tribes like the Iravans, the toody-tappers of Malabar, the Coorgs, the Todas and the Kotas of the Nilgiri Hills. Polyandry facilitates joint-life in the family of the Iravans, mainly an agricultural community.

Polygamy

This system is referred to in the *ṚV.*[52] *AV.*,[53] *TS,*[54] *AB*[55] and ŚB.[56] The art of winning over the husband by one wife is distinctly mentioned in the *Ṛv.*,[57] *Av.*,[58] and *Āpas. Gr. S.*[59] There are lots of references to polygamy in classical Sanskrit literature, specially among the kings and richer section of the society. Kālidāsa says so (*bahuvallabhā rājānaḥ śrūyante*). But neither polyandry nor polygamy was sanctioned by the society to be long-standing. The Dharma school beginning with *Āpas. D.S.*[60] teaches us that one should not marry the second wife, if the first wife is blessed with chastity and progeny. Manu,[61] and Yāj.,[62] prescribe punishment for marrying a second wife after abandoning the first one without sufficient reason. Kauṭilya[63] regulates marriage with a second wife under special circumstances. However, his rules of strīdhana (women's property) in the form of ādhivedanika suggest the prevalence of polygamy in his period. The *Mbh.*,[64] sanctions polygamy and denounces a woman's violation of duty to her first husband: *Na cāpyadharmaḥ Kalyāṇa bahu-patnīkatā nṛṇāṃ/ strīṇām-adharmaḥ su-mahān bhartuḥ pūrvasya laṅghane//*. The inscriptions[65] mention the dedication of Jaina images by ladies, noted in each case as the first wife, indicating thereby the system of polygamy working in the society. A large number of women, mentioned as the mother and step-mothers of the King Śāntamūla-I is a clear proof of the practice of polygamy in the society, Vīrapurisadāta is said to have had five wives, three of whom are cousin sisters. Polygamy was resorted to in case the wife went barren. But it was the fashion of the day when kulīnism triumped in medieval India and even as late as the first half of the present century. It may be noted that polygamy possesses more disadvantages than advantages; hence it has been rejected in civilised societies. It has been declared an offence under Hindu Marriage Act, 1955.

Gotra-exogamy

It is one of the most important restrictions laid down on marriage in ancient India. It means prohibition of marriage within the same clan, probably originating from the spirit of aversion to marry a near kin. When paternity was accepted as a social institution as the natural corollary of individual marriage, people wanted to avoid near blood-relations and to bring new blood into the family or the clan for the betterment of progeny. Some think that the Indo-Aryans had borrowed the idea of sept exogamy from the non-Aryans. It should be noted that the non-Aryans were not like the Indo-Aryans, formed into clans and that they were divided into some totemic groups.[66] These groups were engaged in the intertribal warfare and they were interested in capturing woman from the opponent group as a booty. In fact, the system of securing a wife by capture is still found in a mock capture among some of the aboriginal tribes of India. The Brahmanical gotras also might have had totemic origin, as suggested by the names of some of them like Bhāradvāja, Śāṇḍilya, Kāśyapa, and Vātsya.

The Indo-Iranians did indulge in consanguinous marriages but the Indo-Aryans formulated some ethical principles to regulate marriage. Indiscriminate sex-mating, as referred to in the dialogue-hymn of Yama and Yamī of the *ṚV*,[67] the *AB*[68] and the *ŚB*[69] was looked down upon in the then society. The *ṚV*[70] mentions that marriage took place among strangers who lived at a considerable distance from each other. Thus marriage came to be practised not among the members of the same family or clan but from outside. "The prohibition as to the sameness of gotra in marriage had its origin long before the period of the sūtras in the times of the Brāhmaṇa-works, if not earlier", so says Dr. Kane.[71] The term sagotra is found for the first time in the *Tāṇḍya Brāhmaṇa*[72] (*Sagotrāya brāhmaṇe deyaḥ somapīṭhasyāvidohāya*). Gotra and Pravara systems are fully described in the Sūtra works of Bodhāyana.[73] In the words of Kane[74] "gotra is the latest ancestor or one of the latest ancestors of a person by whose name his family has been known for generations; While pravara is constituted by the sage or sages who lived in the remotest past, who were most illustrious and who are generally the ancestors of the gotra sages or in some cases of the remotest ancestor alone".

The term Gotra is found in the *ṚV*. but not in the sense of descendants of a common patriarchal ancestor.[75] It is used in the *AV*.[76] to mean "a group of persons connected together"; and by this time it might have indicated family relationship. It is only in the period of the Brāhmaṇas that the 'Gotra' system was evolved with the help of pravaras which were religious institutions on the basis of discipleship. Towords the beginning there was only one Gotra, 'Bhṛgu-Aṅgiras' but gradually we find the rise of eight. The Brahmins were taken to be progeny of seven Ṛṣi-s and of Agastya and they declared themselves to be superior to others and asserted their spiritual supremacy over all. The Kṣattriyas might have had their gotras at the beginning but gradually with the supremacy of the Brāhmaṇas they were denied this privilege and they were known by the 'Gotra's of their priests', as stated by Āpastamba.[77] Gautama[78] prohibits marriage with a girl of the same pravara (*a-samāna-pravarai-r vivāhaḥ*), but he is silent about marriage with one of the same gotra. But elsewhere he considers a 'sa-gotra' marriage a great offence as grave as that of violating the bed of one's guru. (*sakhi-sayoni-sagotra-talpasamaḥ*). Āpastamba, as quoted in Udvāha-tattva,[79] declares the child born of such marriage as a caṇḍāla. Bodhāyana ordains cāndrāyaṇa penance in such a marriage. Manu[80] prohibits marriage between the same gotra among the twice-born classes: - *a-sapiṇḍā ca yā mātur asagotrā ca yā pituḥ/ sā praśastā dvijātīnāṃ dārakarmaṇi maithune//*, thus including even the Kṣattriyas and Vaiśyas. However, Āpastamba and Bodhāyana enjoin that by such marriage one loses 'brahminhood' and so it may not be unlikely that Manu means by dvijāti only the brahmins. Yāj.,[81] Viṣṇu[82] and Nārada[83] prohibit marriage with a sagotra girl. Yāj.,[84] as noted above, prescribes penances for violation of this rule. Parāśara whose laws are meant for the Kali age (*kalau pārāśaraḥ smṛtaḥ*) also condemns this practice, but he prescribes some penitentiary rites for the violation of this rule. Medhātithi, while commenting on Manu,[85] declares emphatically that such a marriage, even if held, should be treated as null and void. (*ataḥ sagotrādivivāhaḥ kṛto' pyakṛta eva, evam sagotrāyāḥ na bhāryātvam*). Vijñāneśvara[86] also follows suit. (*sapiṇḍā-samānagotra-samāna-pravarásu bhāryātvam eva notpadyate*). Manu,[87] in the eye of Kullūka (*sagotrāṃ mātu-r-apyeke necchantyudvāha-karmaṇi*) and Medhātithi (*mātulasya sutāṃ caiva mātṛ-gotrāṃ Yathaiva ca*) and Vijñāneśvara commenting on Yāj (1.53): *mātṛ-gotrāmapya-pariṇeyām*, holds the same view. Mādhava, while interpreting Parāśara[88] refers to Yama who speaks of a child born of such marriage as a caṇḍāla. From the above discussion it is evident that "the jurists did not sanction marriage with a sagotra girl". But why? It may be pointed out that the girl might have been married in the third or fourth degree on the mother's side inspite of blood relationship but a sagotra girl, though not having blood-relationship could not be married evidently because 'gotra' institution claims one's descent through the patriarchal line.

Next arises the question of Asapiṇḍa marriage. We come across the term piṇḍa in the *ṚV.*[89] in the sense of 'a part of the body of the sacrificial animal thrown into fire as an offering". Piṇḍa is also used in the *ŚB*[90] to mean "a ball of rice offered to the manes". In the gotra system the father attained a pre-eminent position and his sons are duty-bound to offer piṇḍa to him after his death. This is due to the influence of the doctrine of ancestor worship. The circle of relations, closely connected with the offering of piṇḍa forms a particular group exogamous in character. Āpastamba[91] quotes the following Gāthā: "(Having considered myself) formerly a father, I shall not allow (any longer) my wives (to be approached by other man) since they have declared that a son belongs to the begetter in the world of Yama. The giver of the seed carries off the son after death to Yama's world; therefore they guard their wives, fearing the seed of strangers. Carefully watch over (the procreation) your children lest stranger's seed be sown on your soil. In the next world the son belongs to the begetter, an (imprudent) husband makes the (begetting) children vain (for himself)". Bodhāyana also quotes the same Gāthā with a little variation. This shows the position of paternity in the society and the relation of husband and wife, fidelity between the two being so much stressed upon as to prohibit the levirate system. The 'sapiṇḍa' marriage was prohibited by all the Dharmasūtras and Dharmaśāstras, though with a slight difference in the degree of sapiṇḍatā. Gautama[92] allows marriage after the seventh and fifth generations from the father's and mother's side respectively (*Ūrdhvaṃ saptamāt pitṛ-bandhubhyaḥ and ūrdhvam pañcamāt mātṛ bandhubhyaḥ*). Vasiṣṭha says: *Pañcamīṃ mātṛbandhubhyaḥ saptamīm pitṛ-bandhubhyaḥ*, "(i.e., one should marry a girl) who is not related within five degrees on the mother's side and seven degrees on the father's side". He says nothing about gotra or pravara. Manu[93] recommends a-sapiṇḍā and a-sagotrā girl for marriage and he states that sapiṇḍa-relationship stands upto the seventh generation (*sapiṇḍatā tu puruṣe saptame vinivartate*).[94] Elsewhere,[95] however, he enjoins that piṇḍa should be given to three generations, the fourth is the giver and the relation ceases with him (*Trayānām-udakaṃ Kāryaṃ triṣu piṇḍaḥ pravartate/ caturthaḥ Sampradātaiṣāṃ pañcamo no'papadyate//*). Although he prohibits marriage with relations till the third degree or sāpiṇḍya, we are not sure of his advice to marry in the fourth generation. Yāj.[96] prescribes that the wife should be a-sapiṇḍā and a-samānagotrājā (not of the same piṇḍa and of the same Ṛṣi and gotra) and that she should be 'fifth and seventh removed from the mother and the father respectively' (*pañcamāt saptamād-ūrdhvaṃ mātṛtaḥ pitṛta-s-tathā*), Vijñāneśvara on Yāj. (1.52) explains Sapiṇḍa-relationship as follows: "Sapiṇḍa-relationship arises between two persons through their being connected by particles of one body". Thus the son stands in sapiṇḍa-relationship to his father, because the particles of his father's body have entered the son's body. In the same way a grandson stands in sapiṇḍa-relationship to his grandfather because through the medium of the father the particles of the grandfather's body have entered the grandson's body. The son is a mother's sapiṇḍa because the particles of the mother's body have entered into his own. Likewise the grandson stands in sapiṇḍa-relationship to his maternal grandfather and the rest through his mother. So also is the nephew a sapiṇḍa relation of his maternal aunt's and uncle's and the rest because the particles of the same body (maternal grandfather) have entered into his and theirs. Likewise does he stand in Sapiṇḍa-relationship with paternal uncles and aunts and the rest. So also the wife and the husband are sapiṇḍa-s, because they together beget one body (son). Brothers' wives are sapiṇḍas because they produce the body of sons severally with their husbands who have sprung up from one body. Sapiṇḍa-relationship is, therefore, 'connection with one's body, either immediate or by descent'. Thus sapiṇḍa-relationship may be extended to any number of generations and this is why Yāj. limits it in the next verse (1.53), stated above, for seven generations on the father's side and five on the mother's side. Vijñāneśvara explains it as: "six sapiṇḍa-s beginning with father, six descendants beginning with son and one's self in the seventh", this is with reference to father's side. So on the mother's side, the sapiṇḍas are the ancestors upto the fifth generation beginning with the mother and counting her father, grandfather and others. This explanation agrees with Manu's injunction to the extent that Manu limits sapiṇḍatā within seven generations and also with that of Paiṭhīnasi who enjoins that "one should leave a girl who is fifth from the mother or seventh from the father". But it differs with Paiṭhīnasi's second alternative: "One should leave the girl who is third from the mother and fifth from the father". (*Pañcamīṃ mātṛtaḥ pariharet saptamīṃ pitṛtaḥ trīn mātṛtaḥ pañca pitṛtaḥ vā*). Bālam Bhaṭṭa solves this problem of the second alternative saying that this applies to sons by different mothers belonging to different castes. Vijñāneśvara[97] says that the rules of Vaṣiṣṭha and Paiṭhīnasi mean that they prohibited marriage with girls distant by a lesser number of degrees but they never permitted marriage within the degrees prohibited by Yājñavalkya (*tadapyarvāṅ niṣedhārthaṃ na punas tat prāptyartham iti sarva-smṛtīnāṃ avirodhaḥ*"). He adds that the rules apply in cases of marriage within the same castes (*etacca samāna-jātīye draṣṭavyam*). But in case an ancestor married two wives, one Brāhmaṇa and the other Kṣattriya, the eligibility of marriage among his descendants was regulated by the rule of restricting sapiṇḍa-relationship only upto three degrees and not seven or five (*tri-puruṣameva sāpiṇḍyam iti*). Aparārka explains that the second alternative of Paiṭhīnasi is meant for adopted sons and the like (*dattakādīn putrān pitṛ-pakṣato nivṛtta-sapiṇḍagotrārṣeyān pratyetaducyate pañca pitṛta iti nānyān prati iti*).

Cross-Cousin marriage

This system may be traced even from the *Rv.*[98] (*āyāhīndra patibhir-īlitebhir yajñamimaṃ no bhāgadheyaṃ juṣasva/ tṛptāṃ jahu-mātulasya yoṣā bhaga-s-te paitṛṣvaseyī vapāmiva*".): "Come, O Indra, by commended paths to our sacrifice and partake of your portion. They (the priests) have offered fat seasoned with ghee which they portion as the maternal-uncle's daughter or the paternal-aunt's daughter (is one's lot in marriage)". Kane[99] also refers to the *Śatapatha-Brāhmaṇa* for such practice. The *ŚB* (1, 8, 3, 6) states that "from one and the same man spring both the enjoyer (the husband) and the one to be enjoyed (the wife): for now kinsfolk live sporting and rejoicing together, saying, "In the fourth (or) third man (i.e. generation) we unite". This passage shows that the prohibition of intermarriage between near blood-relations, so rigidly enforced in later times and enjoined by *Bodh. D.S.* (II, 5, 15, 16) was not yet firmly established in the period of the *ŚB*. Harisvāmin remarks that the Kāṇvas allow intermarriage in such cases from the third generation and the Saurāṣṭras from the fourth generation. The above passage of the *ŚB*. shows the possibility of marriage between persons related as either first or second cousins. Gautama[100] declares it to be a custom leading to one's fall (*patitaḥ*). *Bodhāyana D.S.*[101] refers to such a custom of the south and condemns it (*mātulapitṛ-svasṇ-duhitṛ-gamanam ... nādriyate śiṣṭāgama-virodha-darśanāt*). Āpastamba[102] also condemns this sort of marriage. Manu[103] prescribes Cāndrāyaṇa in such cases. Śātātapa is also quoted to have prescribed the same penance in the commentary of Haradatta on *Āpas. D.S.*[104] : *mātulasya sutām-uḍhvā mātṛ-gotrām tathaiva ca samānapravarām caiva dvijaś cāndrāyanaṃ caret.*[105] The Cross-cousin marriage appears to have been in vogue in the period of the *Jātakas*, as evidenced by the Asilakkhana and Mudapāṇi *Jātakas*[106] in which a king is described as giving his daughter in marriage to his sister's son (bhāgineyo). Elsewhere[107] we come across the wicked queen of Padumakumāra who took to a paramour, noted as 'the son of her father's sister'. The prince Vessantara is also said to have married his maternal uncle's daughter, princess Maddī (mātuladuhitaram) in the *Jātaka*.[108] Marriage with the daughter of the mother's sister or the son of the father's brother is rarely noted in the *Jātakas* and so such type of marriage was obviously not the usual practice. The Mahāvagga[109] refers to the common type of cross-cousin marriage between Ajātaśatru and Vajirā. Cross-cousin marriage was also in practice among the Śākyas who never gave their daughters in marriage to another clan; and also among the Mauryas, as evidenced by the *Mahāvaṃśaṭikā* which mentions that Bindusāra's mother was Chandragupta's eldest maternal-uncle's daughter whom he had married.[110] Aśoka's mother was also Maurya princess called Dharmā, a cousin of Bindusāra. The *Mahābodhivaṃśa* (ed. Strong, p. 98) also states that Vidiśā-devī was born in a Śākya clan which had come to Vidiśānagara out of fear of Vidudhava menacing their mother country. That is why Aśoka, while governing Avantī was interested in Devi who was a distant cousin.[111] From Bhāsa's play (Avimāraka) we learn that king Kuntībhoja of Vairantya in Malwa was married with the sister of the king of the Sauvīras who was again married with the sister of Kuntībhoja. Another sister of Kuntībhoja, Sudarśanā was married to the king of Kāśī. Kuntībhoja's daughter, Kuraṅgī was sought after by both the kings of Sauvīra and of Kāsī for their sons but Kuntībhoja decides to offer his daughter to Avimāraka, the son of the king of Sauvīra because he was doubly related, being his sister's son and also his wife's brother's son. Here Avimāraka is shown as marrying his maternal-uncle's daughter who was at the same time his paternal aunt's daughter.

The Mahābhārata refers to such marriages in between Kṛṣṇa and Rukmiṇī, Arjuna and Subhadrā, Pradumna[112] and the daughter of his maternal-uncle, Sahadeva with the daughter of the king of Madra, Śiśupāla and Bhadrā, Parīkṣit and Irāvatī, daughter of Uttarā. These cases indicate the prevalence of the system even in North India. Ajātaśatru is reported in the Buddhist literature to have married Vajirā, his maternal uncle's daughter. Ānanda wanted to marry Uppalavannā, daughter of his paternal sister.[113] Prof. H.C. Chakladar[114] refers to some historical evidences of such marriage: "The Rāṣṭrakūṭa monarch Kṛṣṇa II who reigned during the last part of the ninth and beginning of the tenth century, had as his Mahadevī or Chief Queen, a daughter of the Haihaya Cedi King Kokkala and from them was born Joggattuṇga II who married Lakṣmī, daughter of his maternal uncle Raṇavigraha, a son of Kokkala. From this union sprang up Indra III who again married Vijambā, daughter of Ammanadeva who himself was the son of Arjuna, another son of Kokkala".

The Nagarjunikonda Pillar inscription[115] of the time of Vīrapuruṣadatta (dated 273-274 A.D.) is important from the social point of view. The large number of women, noted as the mother and step-mothers of the King Śāntamūla I is a clear proof of the practice of polygamy in the society. Vīrapuruṣadatta is stated to have five wives of whom three were cousin-sisters, (i) the daughter of Śāntiśrī, his paternal aunt (*apano jāmatukasa*) and (ii & iii) two others, Bappisiri and Ṣaṣṭhi-siri, daughters of Haraśrī, his second paternal aunt. The Nirṇayasindhu[116] states that the Vedic passages, quoted before allow one's marriage with the daughter of a paternal aunt, but such marriage should not be contracted, as these are hateful to the people and because no other passages advise such marriage (*yadyapi pitṛ-svasṛ-kanyodvāhopi prāptas-tathāpyasvargyaṃ loka-vidviṣṭaṃ dharmyam-apyācharen na tu iti niṣedhād vacanāntareṇa tad-udvāhasyavidhānācca na kāryaḥ*). The Smṛticandrikā[117] and Parāśara-Mādhava[118] are also not in favour of such marriage on the same grounds.

Daṇḍin refers to cross-cousin marriage in his works. Arthapāla, son of Kāntimatī is painted as marrying Maṇikarṇikā, daughter of Candraghoṣa, a brother of Kāntimatī.[119] The *ASK*[120] refers to Śūdraka as marrying Yajñadā, daughter of his maternal uncle. Candravarman desired to marry Avantīsundarī, daughter of Mānasāra, who was his sister's father-in-law. According to another tradition Avantīsundarī was Candravarman's cousin. Candravaman was the son of Darpasāra's father's sister. Mānasāra being thus his maternal uncle Avantīsundarī was his cousin. Kane[121] refers to the system of marrying one's niece (own sister's daughter) among the Brāhmaṇas like Deśasthas in Karṇāṭaka and Mysore. In Ramangavda vs Shivaji the Bombay High Court held that such marriage with one's own sister's daughter was invalid among the Brāhmaṇas. Devanabhaṭṭa, himself a southerner is found to have supported cross-cousin marriage. Hemādri also did not prescribe any penance for such marriage. Mādhava followed the suit. According to Devanbhaṭṭa and Mādhava[122] such marriage, if performed in the Brāhma form is valid all over India, Devanabhaṭṭa argues that as soon as girls are married in the Brāhma form, they change their original gotra and sapiṇḍa and so there should be no bar in such cross-cousin marriage. Only in Gāndharva and Āsura forms the change of gotra is not possible; and so such marriage is not allowed. Mādhava, however, insists on local customs being sufficient to make such valid. It is interesting to note that no Smṛti allows marriage between children of two sisters. Devanabhaṭṭa[123] states though there is no harm in such connections, the local customs should be regarded but such marriage should not be encouraged (*Na brūmaḥ śāstrataḥ na parineyeti kintu loka-viruddhatvāt. Yacca dharmyam-api loka-viruddhaṃ tannānuṣṭheyam*). It may not be unlikely that as the matrilineal family traces the descent through mothers, children of two sisters were not allowed to marry. Likewise in the patrilineal family which traces the descent through fathers, children of two brothers were debarred to marry each other. Medhātithi[124] holds that "a person falling in love with the beautiful maternal-uncle's daughter, married her for fear of the king's punishment lest he should be penalised for approaching the girl; Others, however, not knowing the rules, took to the old practice of their ancestors for fear of punishment". (*rūpavatīm mātula-kanyāṃ kāmayamānā rājabhayād ūḍhavantaḥ kanyā-gamana-daṇḍo mābhūditi. Anye tvavidvāṁso yenāsya pitaro yātā ityasya yathāśrutam arthaṃ gṛhītvā dharmo' yam-iti pratipannaḥ*). By the time of Kumārila[125] this system had become a transgression of law.

Cross-cousin marriage outside the families of the Yādavas and the Pāṇḍavas is rarely found in Brahmanical literature. Outside Madhyadeśa, the people of Magadha, Kāśī, Kośala, Mālava, Vidarbha, Surāṣṭra, Sauvīra and Matsya indulged in such marriage. Even at present this practice has become very sporadic among the Aryans except among the Marathi-speaking peoples (Cf. Ghurye, G.S. - *Caste, class and occupation*, pp.40-42). Kappadia's remark deserves our attention - "Cross-cousin marriage is not always conditioned by a particular social fact, while in some cases cross-cousin marriage is associated with inheritance passing to a sister's son and it takes place to implement affection between brother and sister. While in some cases it is associated with the dual organisation of society for marriage, in Brahmanic culture it was tolerated when kinship through the female was not stressed". (*M. & F. in India*, pp. 133-34).

Cross-cousin marriage is an important feature of the Dravidian peoples, as shown by W.H.R. Rivers in his "Marriage of cousins in India". *J.R.A.S.*, 1907 and also by G.S. Ghurye in his *Caste, class and occupation*, p. 128 and *Dual organization in India*, pp. 1-18; and it is not unlikely that it was the product of dual organisation.

The Nāgas of Assam also might have practised marriage with a sister's daughter, as established by Kapadia in his "The matrilineal social organisation of the Nāgas of Assam, section-III".

Marriage was also restricted on the ground of what is known as Viruddha-sambandha, though, of course there is no question of sapiṇḍa-relationship. The Viruddha-sambandha[126] (incompatible relation) arises in cases where the relation between the bride and her groom resembles that of father or mother to the other or of brother and sister, as for example, one's marriage with the daughter of one's wife's sister or the sister of one's paternal uncle's wife. At present, however, such marriage is accepted as valid even among the Brāhmaṇas and Śūdras in Andhrapradesh and Tamilnadu on the basis of Mandlik's Hindu Law.[127]

Among the Muslims, however, marriage with a father's brother's daughter is more or less obligatory; and she is called 'bintaam', i.e. the first wife and it is considered to be offence, if she is neglected. The endogamous rules are also followed by the Muslims. The Sunnis and the Shiahs do not intermarry. The groups like the Vohras, Tais etc. of the Sunnis are also endogamous. Besides, a Saiyad prefers a Saiyad, a Shaikh, a Moghul or a Pathan prefers to marry within the same group. (*Ency. of Islam*, III, 865).

REFERENCES

1. III. 2.1.
2. III. 27.
3. III. 25.
4. III. 29.
5. III. 30.
6. III. 31.

7. III. 32.
8. III. 33.
9. I.245-6.
10. III. 34.
11. *Hindu Marriage Past and Present*, p. 39.
12. III. 53.
13. *Manu*, III. 24.
14. I.60.
15. I.20.14.
16. *Megasthenes and Arrian*. (Mc Crindle, p. 222).
17. II. 21,2.
18. III. 51.
19. Frag. 27.
20. 1, 109, 2.
21. VI, 9.
22. pp. 182 & 187.
23. pp. 67, 85-6.
24. X. 27.2.
25. 1, 20.12.
26. V. 24.
27. V. 38.
28. N. Subrahmanian, p. 291.
29. *Kāmasūtra*, III, 5, 29-30.
30. *DKC*, pp. 67, 85-86, 150 & 163; *ASK*, p. 187.
31. III, 41.
32. *Hist. of Human marriage*, p. 390.
33. III, 23; Cf *Bodh. D.S.* 1.20, 12-13.
34. I, 61.
35. *AŚ*, p. 152.
36. X. 27.12.
37. VII. 66, 73 & 74.
38. V. 32.
39. *Mothers* (by Brifault), Vol. I, pp. 680-681.
40. Polybius, XII, 6; *Mothers*, I, p.693.
41. *Rv*, 1, 119, 5 and *Av*., vi, 82, 2.
42. 1, 167, 4.
43. XIV. 2, 14.

44. XIV. 2.1.
45. XIV. 2.18.
46. XIV. 2.33.
47. *Mbh.* (Ādi), 197-29.
48. II. 10.27.3.
49. 1.26.
50. *ERE*, VIII, p. 453.
51. *Hist. Sketches of S. India*. I, p. 470 and III, p. 4.
52. X, 145; 159, 6; 1, 105, 8.
53. III, 18.
54. VI, 6, 4, 3.
55. 12. 12.
56. XIII. 2, 6.
57. X, 145.
58. III, 18.
59. LX, 6-8.
60. II, 5, 11, 12-13.
61. VIII, 389.
62. 1.74.
63. III, 2.
64. I. 160.36.
65. Lüd.-Nos. 29, 48, 50 & 122 .
66. *Origin of Civilisation and Primitive condition of Man*, p. 94.
67. X, 10.8.
68. 3.33.1.
69. 1.7.4.1.
70. X, 85, 26, 32-33 & 46.
71. *H.D.S.*, II, p. 48.
72. 18, 2, 12.
73. *Bodh.D.S.*, Pravarādhyāya, 54.
74. *H.D.S.*, II. p.497.
75. *Ibid.*, p. 479.
76. V. 21, 3.
77. *Gotra-pravara-nibandha-Kadambam*, pp. 317-318.
78. IV. 2.
79. XXIII, 12, p. 112.
80. III, 5.

81. I, 53.
82. XXIV. 9.
83. XII. 7.
84. III, 231.
85. III, 7.
86. Mitākṣarā on Yāj. I, 53.
87. III, 5.
88. X. 5.
89. I. 162.19.
90. II, 4, 2, 24; Cf. *TB* II, 3, 8, 2 *Nirukta*, III, 4-5.
91. *Āpas. D.S.*, II, 6, 13, 6.
92. IV. 3 & 5.
93. III, 5.
94. III, 80.
95. IX. 186.
96. I, 52-53.
97. Mitākṣarā on Yāj. I. 53.
98. Aufrecht, Vol. II, p. 672; Kane, *H.D.S.* II, p. 461 fn.
99. *H.D.S.* II, p. 461.
100. *Gaut. D.S.*, XXI. I.
101. 1.1, 19, 26.
102. II, 5, 11, 16.
103. XI, 170-173.
104. II, 5, 11, 16.
105. *Harivaṃśa*, p. 299 and p. 304.
106. *J.I.*, p. 457; II, p. 327.
107. J., II, p. 119.
108. J., IV. p. 49 and VI, 486.
109. VIII, 1, 2, 3.
110. *Aśoka and his inscriptions* ed. B.M. Barua, pt. I and II, p. 38.
111. *J.O.I*, Vol. XX, Nos. 1-4 (1970-71), p. 120.
112. *Harivaṃśa*, pp. 299 & 304.
113. *I.H.Q.* II pp. 564-65, Cf. *Mahāvaṃśa* (ed. Geiger), p. 58. *IHQ*, II, p. 665.
114. *Social life in Anc. India*- A Study on Vātsyāyaṇa's Kāmasūtra, (1976) Delhi, p. 133.
115. *E.I.*, XXI, pp. 63-64 and XXXV, pp. If.

116. III (Pūrvārdha), p. 286
117. I, p. 71.
118. I, 2, p. 65.
119. *D.K.C.*, p. 136.
120. p. 201.
121. *H.D.S.*, II, pt. 1, p. 467. Cf. Mandlik's *Hindu Law*, p. 425.
122. *Parāśara-Mādhava*-I, 2, p. 469.
123. *Smṛticandrikā*, I, p. 191.
124. On Manu, II, 18.
125. On Jaiminī 1.3.7.
126. Āśvalāyana-Gṛhha-pariśiṣṭa, 22.
127. Pp. 484-485.

PART - II

CHAPTER - IV

Intercaste Marriage in Ancient India

The problem of intercaste marriage requires a careful study of the caste system with its bearing on marriage. Several scholars consider caste system as a social phenomenon which originates from the Vedic period in a different manner. Sidney Low[1] speaks highly of its beneficent aspect as "the main cause of the fundamental stability and contentment by which Indian society has been braced up for centuries against the shocks of politics and the cataclysms of Nature". Abbe Dubois[2] considers the caste system as "the happiest effort of their legislation". Others like Sherring[3] look upon it as "the most baneful, hard-hearted and cruel social system". No rose is without thorns. The old ideals and institutions are being replaced by new ones by the impact of western culture and by other forces. Now caste means a matter of marriage and to a certain degree, of food and drink. As regards occupation, now-a-days there is little restriction castewise, as was once in the past. The caste is known by two terms Varṇa and jāti. The earliest reference to four castes, Brāhmaṇas, Rājanyas (Kṣattriyas), Vaiśyas and Śūdras is found in the Puruṣasūkta.[4] The *Avesta* also speaks of such four classes of ancient Iranian people, Atharvas (priest), Rathestas (charioteers or warriors), Vastriya Fshouyanta (agriculturists and artisans) and Hiuti (serfs). These class-distinctions of the Vedic Aryans and the ancient Iranians lead us to infer that the Aryans must have brought them even from their original homes elsewhere. Of course, Zarathrusta has been painted in the Avesta as the first priest, warrior and agriculturist and so we may think that the class-distinction in ancient Iran was flexible. In the earliest phase of the *Ṛgveda* two rival camps of the Ārya-s and Dāsa-s or Dasyus are heard of as existing, differing not only in the colour of their skins but also in worship, speech and bodily appearance. In India of the Ṛgvedic period the class-or more seriously caste-distinction is rarely heard of except in the tenth Maṇḍala, Puruṣasūkta which is taken by some scholars as an interpolation. However, the fourfold castesystem, if any was invented in the later Ṛgvedic period. Winternitz[5] remarks: "Certainly there were warriors and priests but of an exclusive warrior caste there is in the Ṛgveda as little mention as of one or several lower castes of farmers, cattle raiders, merchants, artisans and labourers". However, it seems that the four varṇas were four groups of people, classified according to their professions; and all these four taken together constituted the organic whole of the social structure. From the duties assigned to the four varṇas in the Brāhmaṇa texts we learn that the Brāhmaṇas were the spiritual guides, the Kṣattriyas were the temporal rulers in charge of administration and protection of the people, the Vaiśyas looked after trade and agriculture and the Śūdras served the upper three castes. While the Aryans moved from the Indus valley towards the Gangetic plain and further eastward and southward, they met the stiffest resistance from the non-aryan tribes who were conquered and gradually converted into serfs, designated as Dāsa-s or Dasyus swelling the group of the Śūdras. The Aryan invaders married very often the girls of the Dravidian and pre-Dravidian people. It may be pointed out that the Indo-Aryans who were the authors of Vedic Sanskrit literature have been regarded as belonging to the Nordic stock. They came to the land of the Dāsas, i.e. the pre-aryans. These Dāsa-s were defeated and reduced to slavery and many of them met death at the hands of the victorious Aryan Chiefs and their women also were either engaged as slaves or concubines. Thus, there was fusion of the Aryan and non-Aryan groups. The Vasiṣṭhas were noted in the *Rv.* as svityam (white), whilst the Kāṇvas, as dark (Śvāva or Kṛṣṇa-vii, 33.1 and X.31.11). The dark Ṛṣis were evidently the issues of the fusion. The marriage of Vimada, a protege of Aśvins with the daughter of Purumitra, obviously of the Puru tribe also indicates such intermixture of blood. And as its natural corollary we come across the rise of the

Kurus in the post-Ṛgvedic stage out of the mixture of the Purus and the Bharatas. The very name 'Dīrghatamas' of the sage, known by his metronymic also indicates the flow of non-Nordic blood in his vein, because the Aryan society was positively patriarchal in character. This interracial interaction resulted in the introduction of the cerebral consonants into Indo-Aryan language as early as the Ṛgvedic period as well as in the dark complexion of many Aryans belonging to the Kṣattriya class. The intermediate grades of complexion, caused by interracial marriage led ultimately to the rise of the four varṇas instead of two.[6] The ṛc[7] (*agastyaḥ khanamānaḥ khanitraiḥ prajāmapatyaṃ valam icchamānaḥ ubhau varṇāvṛṣi-r-ugraḥ puposa satyā deveṣvāśiṣo jagāma*) shows distinctly the existence of only two varṇas, Ārya and Dāsa in the early Vedic age. There is no doubt that the Āryas did not like marriage-alliance with the Śūdras. In *Vāj. Sam.* illicit connections between Ārya and Śūdra are severely reprobrated. However, in the Vedic age when a member of one class could thus easily be a member of another class, the prevalence of marriage between these classes goes without saying. We have numerous instances of marriage between Brāhmaṇa and Kṣattriya classes. The *AV.*[8] shows that the Brāhmaṇa is glorified as the best of all husbands of a woman belonging to all classes (*Uta yat patayo daśa striyāḥ pūrve abrāhmaṇāḥ/ Brahmā ced-adhastamagrahit sa eva patirekadhā/ / Brāhmaṇa eva pati-r-ṇa rājanyo na Vaiśyaḥ/ tat Sūryaḥ pravruvanneti pañcabhyo mānavebhyaḥ/ /*).

Yayāti married Devayānī, daughter of the ṛṣi Uśanas-Śukra. The ṛṣi Cyavana[9] married Sukanyā, daughter of King Saryāta. Cyavana's descendant Apnavān married Ruci, daughter of King Nahuṣa. His descendant Ṛicika married Satyavatī, daughter of King Gāthin of Kānyakubja. Their son Jamadagni married the Kṣattriya Lady Reṇukā. Agastya married Lopamudrā, daughter of King Vidarbha. Another instance of intercaste marriage is that of Vatsa,[10] who, when suspected of being the son of a Śūdra woman, had to establish his purity by a fire-ordeal. In the later Vedic society classes were crystallised into castes and by the end of the Vedic age castes tended to be absolutely hereditary. The ṛc[11] mentions Kakṣīvant as son of the female slave named Uśij. The Bṛhaddevatā[12] shows how in the sacrifice of Dārbhya Rathavīti, Archanānasa, son of Atri, was invited as a priest, his son Śyāvāśva also went to assist. Śyāvāśva wanted to marry the beautiful daughter of the king Rathavīti, but the queen disagreed because he was not a seer of the Mantra. At last when the Mantra *'ya iṃ vahante'* was revealed to him, he was accepted as a competent groom. The statement in *ŚB*[13] - *Śūdrā yat āryajārā*, i.e. "a Śūdra woman who is the concubine of some male belonging to the Ārya class" shows the distinction of the Śūdras, from the Aryan community. The Vaiśyas were more honourable than the Śūdras and they were entitled to 'Upanayana' and thus included into the group of three higher castes known as dvija-s. They are described in the *Ait. Brāhmaṇa*[14] as paying tax, being lived on by another and oppressed at will. (*anyayasya valikṛt anyasyādyaḥ yathākāmaṃ jeyaḥ*). The śūdras on the other hand, are noted as "servants of another, to be evicted at will and to be slain at will", showing thereby that the śūdras had no right of property or security of life against the king or the noblity in general. The Brāhmaṇas and the Kṣattriyas were two superior classes and their mutual cooperation was essential for the upkeep and smooth running of the society and the state. The *Ait. Br.*[15] mentions two lower castes, nīcyas and apācya-s. The ancedote of Viśvāmitra, refers to various outcastes such as Andhras, Puṇḍras, Śabaras, Pulindas and Mutivas—all people living outside the Aryan belt in the age of the Brāhmaṇas. The tale of Kavaṣa, son of Iluṣa in the *AB*[16] tells us how even a bastard, born of a maid-servant received the favour of Sarasvatī. Mahidāsa, author of *AB.*, a śūdra is another instance of the rise of the śūdras whose superiority was accepted even by the higher castes. Such enlightened persons belonging to the lower castes were obviously upgraded in social rank only through knowledge. Birth or heredity determines one's caste. It may be pointed out that intercaste marriage in the Vedic age took the shape of hypergamy. In the Ṛgvedic age people of the priestly class are said to have married girls of royal families; as for example, Cyavana Śvāvāśva or Vimada. Instances of Kṣattriyas marrying Brāhmaṇa girls were not unknown, as for example, king Svanaya Bhāvayavya's beloved wife was an Āṅgirasī.[17] The *AV.*[18] glorifies the Brāhmaṇa as the best husband for women of all classes. However, it leads us also to infer that the Brahmin women sometimes held contrary views and they had to be reclaimed from persons of other castes with the help of the king. The *TB*[19] and *ŚB*[20] mention the Vaiśiputras of the early Brāhmaṇas. The frequent mention of dāsī-s in the Vedic literature shows that dāsī-s came into contact with the Aryan masters and as a result dāsīputras became so frequent in the then society.

The word ayogu in VS,[21] if related with the āyogava of the Smṛti-s means the Ārya (Vaiśya) woman married to a śūdra, as enunciated by Manu in X. 12. The *Āśvalāyana Gṛhya Sūtra*[22] records the old tradition that the family slave, like the brother-in-law of the widow is entitled to marry the widow of his master.

Lāṭyāyana-śrauta-sūtra[23] enjoins that in the Daśapeya sacrifice ten priests would drink soma after mentioning ten names beginning with father, grandfather etc. and also ten names beginning with mother, grandmother etc. If anyone is found to be a non-Brahmin on the mother's side she should be rejected and ten names are to be uttered accordingly. The *Drāhyāyana Ś.S.* enjoins about this sacrifice that the son of a non-Brahmin woman was also regarded as a Brahmin and fit to be a priest.[24] The question of one's birth was gradually superceded by knowledge and conduct, as reflected in the Upaniṣadic and post-Vedic age and confirmed by the Dharma school. The Lord Kṛṣṇa declares emphatically in the *Gītā*[25]: *Cāturvarṇyaṃ mayā sṛṣṭaṃ guṇakarmavibhāgaśaḥ*, i.e., quality and conduct and not birth determines one's caste. The Śatarudrīya hymn of the *Vāj. Saṃ.*[26] mentions about seventy professions of life, each meant for a particular caste in ancient India. These various sub-castes emerged even as early as the period of the VS. as a result of mixture of castes. Besides, the same source refers to some out-castes and semi-aryan tribes, such as, Niṣāda-s, Baiṇḍas, Kaivartas, Mārgavas (sons of a huntsman), Kirātas, Jambhaka (flesh-eating tribe), Paulkasa (son born of a Niṣāda father and a Kṣattriya mother) and Caṇḍālas. P.V. Kane[27] also thinks that division of labour in the background of various arts and crafts led to the rise of different sub-castes, based on occupations even before the close of the Vedic age. While the *Gītā* was harping on the theory of Varṇa, as noted above, the earlier jurists of India like the writers of Dharmasūtras and Dharmaśāstras strongly advocated the jāti theory. D.R. Bhandarkar[28] shows how the foreign tribes infiltrated into India in the historical period and were gradually Aryanised and admitted into the frame-work of caste-system. The *Mahābhārata*[29] pronounces in clearcut terms:—

nayoni-r-nāpi saṃskāro na śrutam naca santatiḥ/kāraṇāni dvijatvasya vṛttam-eva hi kāraṇam//. That means, neither birth nor the rites of sacraments nor learning nor offspring can be considered as grounds for conferring upon on the dignity of a twice-born person. Indeed, conduct is the only ground. It refers to the rise of a śūdra into a Brāhmaṇa and that of a Vaiśya into a Kṣattriya.[30] Two sons of Nābhāgariṣṭha originally Vaiśyas were promoted into the status of Brāhmaṇa-s, as referred to in the *Harivaṃśa*.[31] Thus we find that both the Varṇa and Jāti theories were operating side by side in the ancient society. Considered from the economic stand point each caste may be taken to be a trade-union. Each looked after the interests of its own group of people. Definitely the castesystem must have been a necessary phenomenon in the history of the growth of the Indian society. The Brahmins attained the supreme position in the society not only for their intellectual and spiritual wealth, but also for the sacrifices they had made. Unlike the priests elsewhere in other parts of the world, the Brahmins took to the life of austerities and renunciation. They did not necessarily seek the throne, though in the historical period we find the rise of Brahmin kings under special circumstances. Life of pleasure was a forbidden fruit to them.[32]

The caste-system allowed the development of each caste in a democratic way, the functions or duties being well-defined as reflected in the Brāhmaṇas and Dharmasūtras. Each group looked after its own interests and was allowed to formulate laws for regulating the life and conduct of its own and instead of undue competition each class was engaged in its own vocations and attained hereditary skill.

In course of time caste-system took the shape of rigidity in place of flexibility and caste-heirarchy brought about some sort of disruption into social life. The supremacy of Brāhmaṇa-s was challenged by other castes, specially the Kṣattriyas as early as the Vedic period, subsequently in the heydey of the rise of Buddhism and Jainism, and then by the śūdras during the ascendency of the Nandas. Kauṭilya[33] regards the śūdras as "ārya-prāṇam" (life-breath of the Āryas). Aśoka removed all social inequalities and preached "equality of punishment" (daṇḍasamatā) and "equality of law" (Vyavahāra-samatā). He treated all his subjects as his sons. The Brahmins lost undue privileges and "Aśoka built a bureaucracy without a varṇa-basis". Then again during the Suṅgas and particularly the Guptas the society witnessed the revival of Brahmanism.

Senart[34] contends that caste in its modern sense did not exist in the Vedic age. Kane[35] remarks rightly that "the practices as to marrying outside one's varṇa and taking food had not become as rigid as cast-iron as they became in medieval times". The intercaste marriage was in fashion as early as the period of the Ṛgveda, as noted above, specially in the days when caste system was at a fluid stage. The three higher professional castes were gradually known as dvija in the later Vedic age; and the non-aryans were absorbed in the framework of castes as Śūdras. Towards the beginning the fluidity of the castesystem proved to be no bar to inter-marriage by courtship. But in proportion to the rigidity of the caste system and the spirit of antagonism prevailing among various castes, barriers of intermarriage proved to be too strong to be crossed over. But still the stories of Kavaṣa, Ailūṣa[36] and Mahīdāsa in the *Ait. Brāh.* indicate the practice of such irregular unions. Kavaṣa Ailūṣa was driven out from the sacrifice on the Sarasvatī with the words "Oh, son of a female slave, you are a rogue and not a brāhmaṇa; how did you take the dikṣā (initiation) as one of us" and he was carried off to a desert so that he would die of thirst there. But when tormented by thirst, he "saw" the hymn (*ṚV*, X. 30) and Sarasvatī came to him. The *ŚB*[37] refers to the Brahmin Cyavana marrying the Kṣattriya girl Sukanyā, daughter of King Śaryāta. The *Bṛhad-devatā*,[38] while interpreting the ṛcs (V. 61, 17-19) mentions the marriage of the Brahmin Śyāvāsa with the daughter of a Kṣattriya Rathavīti Dārbhya. The king had three wives belonging to three castes. The expression *Śūdrā yad-ārya-jārā na poṣāya dhanāyatīti tasmād-Vaiśīputraṃ nābhiṣiñcati*[39] proves such illicit unions between a member of the upper caste and a Śūdra girl. The remark that "he does not anoint (as king) the son of the Vaiśya woman" suggests that a king might have married a Vaiśya girl but her son would not have the Vedic coronation ceremony performed on him. Thus the Aryans were always conscious of their pedigree and they put great stress on the purity of the breed but still we find instances of mixed castes born of cross-breeding between various castes and sub-castes. Some mixed castes like Rathakāras or chariotwrights won responsible position in the society, obviously because chariots were the main conveyances for traffic, trade, warfare, hunting etc.

We have noted above that varṇa breeds the idea of a class on the basis of race, culture, character and profession. But the word jāti, derived from the root jan lays emphasis on birth and heredity. It is hardly met with in the sense of a caste in the Vedic literature. The *Nirukta*[40] mentions it in the sense of a caste (*agniṃ citvā na rāmānupeyāt. Rāmā - ramaṇāyopeyate na dharmāya Kṛṣṇajātīyā*), when it says that after Agnicayana, building of a fire-altar, one should not approach a rāmā (for sexual intercourse): rāmā is one who is approached only for sexual pleasure and not for accumulation of merit, she is of a dark caste. Obviously Kṛṣṇajātīyā means a woman of the śūdra caste. Vasiṣṭha[41] uses almost the same words save and except Kṛṣṇavarṇā in place of Kṛṣṇajātīyā, Viśvarūpa on Yaj.[42] refers to these words as a Brāhmaṇa-text. (*Kṛṣṇa-varṇīyā rāmā ramaṇāyaivopeyate iṭi brāhmaṇa vādaḥ*). Pāṇini uses the word 'jāti' in the sense of a caste (*jātyantācca vandhuni*). Thus the caste system developed in course of time on the basis of heredity. The Dharmasūtras and later on the Dharmaśāstras refer to numerous castes and subcastes on the mixture of varṇas (*varṇaśaṅkara*), evidently the products of intercaste marriage. The myths of anuloma and pratiloma issues like Magadha, Niṣāda etc. invented by the writers of the Dharma School suggest the gradual Aryanisation of various non-aryan or aboriginal tribes or even the incorporation of alien people into the Aryan community. The children born of such inter-caste marriage were generally looked down upon in the contemporary society. Anuloma means the union between a male of a higher varṇa and a female of a lower one; whereas pratiloma means just the reverse, the union between the male of a lower varṇa and a female of the higher order. These two words hardly occur in the Vedic literature in the sense of intercaste marriages. The pratiloma is first heard of in the *Bṛhadāraṇyaka upa.*[44] in the context of a Brāhmaṇa's approach to a Kṣattriya for the Highest knowledge (*Saho vācājātaśatruḥ pratilomam caited yad/ brāhmaṇaḥ Kṣattriyam-upeyād brahma me vyakṣatīti*). From this we may infer that pratiloma and anuloma might have been used in the sense of intercaste marriages also in the period of the earlier upaniṣads. Pāṇini[45] also teaches us the formation of these words. As a result of wide prevalence of such practices in the society of the Upaniṣadic period the authors of Dharmasūtras had to recognise them. Of course, the jurists were always in favour of one's marriage within the same caste (*savarṇa-vivāha*). The anuloma-marriage is again preferred to the pratiloma one, evidently because of the more important position of the husband in the patriarchal society. Āpastamba[46] was however, against even the anuloma marriage: *pūrvavatyām asaṃskṛtāyāṃ varṇāntare ca maithune doṣaḥ, tatrāpi doṣavān putra eva*, i.e. the sexual intercourse with a woman who has been married by another or on whom the sacramental rites of marriage are not performed, or who belongs to another caste, is condemned, and the son (and not the daughter), born of such a union is condemned (through the sin of the parents). The *Hiraṇyakeśin Gṛhyasūtra*[47] also holds the same view. Gautama[48] speaks of pratilomaja as dharmahīna, devoid of religious rites. The hierarchical order of the society was always regarded, while the rules of marriage were framed. Bodhāyāna[49] prescribes that the Brahmin might have four wives from four varṇas, a Kṣattriya three, a Vaiśya two and a Śūdra only one. But the śūdra wife of the males of the higher castes was always looked down upon. Gautama excludes the husband of a śūdra woman from the list of invitees in a Śrāddha ceremony. (of *Viṣṇu Dh. S.*, 24, 1-4).The *Mahābhārata* refers to anuloma marriages as in Parāśara's marriage with Satyavati,[50] Cyavana's with Sukanyā,[51] Ṛcika's with Gādhikanyā,[52] Ṛṣyaśṛṅga's with Śāntā,[53] Agastya's with Lopamudrā[54] and Jamadagni's with Reṇukā.[55] The cases of pratiloma marriage are also equally denounced in the *Mahābhārata*, as in cases of Yayāti and Devayānī[56] and Duṣyanta and Śakuntalā.[57] Yayāti, the Kṣattriya king did not agree to the proposal of marriage, offered by Devayānī, daughter of Śukra, the Brahmin: (*Viddhyauśanasi bhadraṃ te na tvām-arho' smi bhāvini/ a-vivāhyā hi rājāno Devayāni pitu-s-tava* - Adi, 81, 18-30), but accepted her when he had the assurance from her father that Śukra would redress the wrong, if any. Vidura[58] would have married the Kṣattriya daughter if he so desired but he married the Pāraśavī daughter of the King Devaka (*atha pāraśavīm kanyāṃ Devakasya mahīpateḥ*). In the Śakuntalā episode also we find Duṣyanta hesitating to propose to marry Śakuntalā, taking her first to be the daughter of a Brāhmaṇa but when he had learnt of her heredity, he proposed to marry her. The svayaṁvara ceremony of Draupadī also confirms the practice of intercaste marriage in the then society. Suitors of various castes attended the assembly. Even Karṇa went there as a claimant but Draupadī[60] announced aloud- "I won't choose the son of a sūta (*Dṛṣṭvā tu tām Draupadī vākyam-uccai-y-jagāda nāhaṃ varayāmi sūtam*)". Karṇa was not prevented by any one, even by Dhṛṣṭadyumna to convene, though he was known as a Sūta's son. This leads us to infer that the pratiloma-marriage though denounced, was not out of practice in the society. Besides, heroism or skill in fighting was accepted as a bid for svayaṁvara marriage. Hence it is difficult to think of any bar of caste in matters of marriage. Śāntanu knew Satyavatī to be the daughter of a fisherman. He had no doubt about legibility of his marrying her and approached Dāsarāja for the hand of his daughter.[61] This fact also shows that anuloma-marriage was not denounced in the society. The śūdra wife of a twice-born was, though in vogue, condemned and such a union was rarely approched (*ahosvidantatonaṣṭam śrāddham śudrīpatāviva*).[62] Elsewhere[63] we learn of a Brāhmaṇa, born in Madhyadeśa, living with a Śūdra wife, particularly a punarbhū, i.e. previously married with another person (*madhyadeśa-prasuto' ham vāso me śabarālaye*). Somewhere else[64] a Brāhmaṇa speaks of his wife belonging to the Niṣāda caste (*Niṣādī mama bhāryeyaṃ nirgacchatu mayā saha*). We come across controversial opinion about the marriage of a śūdra woman with a twice-born in the *Mahābhārata*. Some think that a śūdra wife may be accepted only for sexual pleasure, but her issue will not be entitled to perform the Śrāddha ceremony; whereas others opine that a śūdra wife of a twice-born is highly condemned (*ratyartham-api śudrā syānnetyāhu-r-aparejanāḥ apatya-janma śūdrāyāṃ na praśaṃsanti Sādhavaḥ*).

It is interesting to note that the issues of such intercaste marriage were recognised in the society, sometimes by their fathers and sometimes by their mother's castes. The sons of Devayānī were never recognised as Brahmins, whereas Kṛṣṇa-dvaipāyana, though born of a Kṣattriya's daughter, reared by a fisherman was accepted as a Brāhmaṇa in the society. But Vidura, though born of a Brahmin father was known as śūdra because his mother was a śūdra. There was a general rule in the society to recognise the issue of the intercaste marriage as belonging to the caste of his or her mother, as evidenced by the *Mbh.*[66] (*bhāryā-s-catasro viprasya dvayo-r-ātmā prajāyate/ ānu-purvyād-dvayo-r-hīnau mātṛ-jātyau prasūyatah//*), though, however, this rule was not always followed in practice.

The *Mbh.* refers to the marriage of a devatā, Yakṣa, rakṣah, nāga, suparṇa and others with a human being. Evidently devatā, Yakṣa etc., these terms were used to mean men of different categories, most probably including even the non-aryans and tribal people of the age. The marriages of Śāntanu with Gaṅgā, of Jaratkāru Ṛṣi with Jaratkāru, sister of Vāsukī, of Bhīma with

Hiḍimbā, of Arjuna with Ulūpī and of Maharṣi Mandapāla with Śārangī draw our attention to intercaste or inter-racial unions in the society. Vāsukī, King of Nāgas is said to have called Bhīma as dauhitradauhitra[67] (*tadā dauhitra-dauhitraḥ pariṣvaktaḥ supīḍitam*). The term hīna-yoni-dhṛta,[68] used with reference to one of the twelve sons proves one's marriage with a woman belonging to an inferior (śūdra) caste. Elsewhere the *Mbh.*[69] mentions additional eight types of sons, over and above twelve, and these eight are evidently products of intercaste marriage. That the maidservants were also regarded as wives of their masters is indicated in the expressions *Kuru-Vaṃśa-Vivardhanaḥ* and *Kurunandanaḥ* with reference to Vidura[71] (*"jajñire deva-garbhābhāḥ Kuru-vaṃśa-vivardhanaḥ and Viduraḥ Kuru-nandanaḥ"*). Nīlakaṇṭha, while commenting on Mbh. (Ādi, 106, 32) says that the mother of Vidura who was but a maidservant, was accepted as the wife of Vicitravīrya. (*Kṣetratvaṃ dāsyā api ityanenaiva gamyate iti kecit*). Vidura, however, inspite of his high learning and wisdom, introduced himself to be a śūdra, not competent to teach spiritual sciences.[72] (*Śūdra-yonāvahaṃ jāto nāto' nyad-vaktum-utsahe*). The *Mbh.*[73] refers to various mixed castes, viz, Atiratha, Ambaṣṭha, Ugra, Vaidehaka, Śvapāka, Pukkasa, Niṣāda, Sūta, Māgadha, Madranābha, Āhiṇḍaka, Carmakāra, Saupāka, and others, each born of parents by intercaste marriage; and the same source mentions greed, desire, and ignorance of varṇa as the causes leading to the rise of such mixed castes.

The position of progeny born of such intercaste marriages indicates how these marriages were accepted in the society. The children, born of anuloma by the wife of the next lower varṇa had more or less equal status with that of the svavarṇa marriage, whereas children born of pratiloma were condemned in the society and they lost even the right of inheritance.

Gautama[74] refers to six anuloma castes- Svavarṇa, Ambaṣṭha, Ugra, Niṣāda, Dauṣmanta, and Pāraśava and also to six pratiloma castes—Sūta, Vaidehaka, Caṇḍāla, Māgadha, Kṣattāra and Āyogava, showing thereby the wide prevalence of intercaste marriage in the society. He speaks of others' opinions that the Brāhmaṇī produces Brāhmaṇa, Sūta, Māgadha and Caṇḍāla in connection with four Varṇas inhierarchical order, Brāhmaṇa and others, that a Kṣattriya produces Mūrdhāvaṣikta, Kṣattriya, Dhīvara, and Pukkasa in connection with a Brāhmaṇa and others in respective order; that a Vaiśya produces Bhṛjjakaṇṭha, Māhiṣya, Vaiśya and Vaideha and that a Śūdra produces Pāraśava, Yavana, Karaṇa and Śūdra in connection with Brāhmaṇa and others. Bodhāyana (i, 1.29) refers to Āryāvarta, the land of the Nordic Aryans, called the śiṣṭa-s but he mentions that the people, surrounding this region like a semi-circle, of Avantī, Aṇga, Magadha, Surāṣṭra, Dakṣiṇāpatha and Sindhu-Sauvīra were of mixed origin (*Saṃkīrṇa-yonayaḥ*), indicating obviously their heterogenous elements, away from Aryan culture. The brāhmaṇas of Magadha are ridiculed as brahmabandhu in the *Śrautasūtra*, but noted with respect in the *Śāñkhāyana Āraṇyaka*. From this we may infer that the Brāhmaṇas of Magadha were mixing with the aboriginal elements, as a result of which the latter were gradually Aryanised. Bodhāyana[75] mentions a few more mixed castes viz., Rathakāra, Śvapāka, Vaiṇa and Kukkuṭa. He holds that the progeny of a male marrying a girl of the next descending order belongs to the varṇa of the father. Āpastamba[76] was dead against the system of intercaste marriage and hence he speaks of only three mixed castes, viz, Caṇḍāla, Paulkasa and Vaiṇa.

Vasiṣṭha[77] states that a Śūdra produces a Caṇḍāla in a Brāhmanī and Antyāvasāyī in a Kṣattriyā or Vaiśyā, that a Vaiśyā, produces Rāṃaka in a Brāhmaṇī and Pukkaśa in a Kṣattriyā and a Kṣattriyā produces Sūta in a Brāhmaṇī. He condemns the pratilomaja-s as devoid of qualities and customs. He speaks of the children of a Śūdra by any of the three higher castes as Niṣāda or Pāraśava. Vasiṣṭha D.S. (1.25-27) does not allow the Āryas including Vaiśyas also to marry a girl of a Śūdra caste and includes among those unfit for invitation to a Śrāddha dinner a Brāhmaṇa who is a śūdrāpati (XV. 18). J.H. Hutton (*Caste in India*, ch. X, pp. 150-151) attributes superiority of anuloma sons to pratiloma ones to the impact of patrilineal invaders on an indigenous matrilineal population and contends that the matrilineal system was once much more widely distributed than it is now. Kosambi refers to "aboriginal matriarchy" and adds that "non-aryan brahmins are called sons of their mothers by name" (Introduction to the *Study of Indian History*, ch. IV, p. 92). In such a society the issue of patrilineal father and matrilineal mother would have status and kinship, with both his parents' families and would inherit from both. Even the issue of patrilocal and matrilocal marriage would receive advantage from at least one side. The laws of inheritance in the Dharmaśāstras, providing share, though unequal, to an anuloma son, born of śūdra prove this point. But the offspring of an immigrant patrilineal woman by an indigenous matrilineal male would have no place with either of the parents and with no claims to kinship or inheritance his status would inevitably tend to be degraded.

Manu[78] speaks highly of marriage within the same caste. However, he has sanctioned anuloma marriage, as evidenced by the fact that "the sons, begotten by twice-born men on wives of the next lower caste are declared to be similar to their father but blamed on account of the fault (inherent) in their mothers" (*Strīsvanantara-jātāsu dvijair-utpāditān sutān sadṛśān-eva tān-āhur-mātṛ-doṣa-vigarhitān*)". But he resents marriage with a śūdra girl of the twice-born and he says emphatically that the son of a Śūdra by the twice-born is not entitled to inherit the paternal property[79] (*brāhmaṇa-Kṣattriya-viśām śūdra-putro na rikthabhāk*). He speaks of the son of a Vaiśya by Brāhmaṇa as 'Ambaṣṭha'. He designates the issue of a Śūdra girl by a Brāhmaṇa as Niṣāda or Pāraśava and by a Kṣattriya as Ugra, possessed of cruel or evil customs and movements (*Krūrācāra-vihāra-vān*) and he declares all the six anulomajas, though he has actually named only the three, as inferior (apasadāḥ) to sons of Svavarṇa marriage. While Bodhāyana[80] mentions the sons begotten by one on women of the next lower caste as Svavarṇa-s (*tāsu putrāḥ svavarṇānantarāsu svavarnāḥ*), Manu speaks of them as sadṛśa (equal) but condemned for their mother's fault, thus pointing out their degraded status in the society.

Manu refers to the issues by pratiloma marriage, viz, Sūta born of a Kṣattriya in a Brahmin girl, Māgadha and Vaideha, born of a Vaiśya in a Kṣattriya and Brahmin girl respectively and Āyogava, Kṣattā and Caṇḍāla, born of a Śūdra in a Vaiśya, Kṣattriya and Brāhmaṇa girl respectively. These last three are called Varṇasañkara and they were the worst of all men' in the society in the eye of Manu[81] *(adhamo nṛṇām)*. Manu mentions Āvṛta as the product of the marriage between a Brahmin male and an Ugra girl, Ābhira as that of the union between a Brahmin male and an Ambaṣṭha girl and Dhigvana as that of the marriage between a Brahmin male and an Āyogava girl; and he speaks of them as polluted by the demerit of their mothers. The pratilomaja-s, mentioned above, and others like Pukkaśa, Kukkuṭaka and Svapāka are all equally abominable,[82] and termed Saṃkīrṇayoni. It is interesting to note that Manu makes a nice distinction between varṇa-saṅkara and saṇkīrṇayoni, Varṇa-saṅkara is the product of the intermixture of blood between different varṇa-s and also of the breach of discipline of the society, as for example, sagotra marriage, marriage in cases where marriage is not permissible and non-performance of rites like sacred-thread ceremony and other obligatory rites.[83] On the contrary, those born of anuloma and pratiloma marriage as a result of union for mutual attraction are termed saṁkīrṇayoni. Medhātithi on Manu (V. 88) explains saṁkarajāta as pratiloma-s like Āyogava (*Saṃkarajāta itaretara-jāti-vyatikareṇa pratiloma āyogavādayaḥ*). The anuloma-s are also mixed castes but they have the castes of their mothers (*mātṛ-jātīyatvāt*), hence Manu does not use the term saṁkīrṇayoni in connection with them, but he means by this term only those born of union of pratiloma and anuloma. (*Vyabhicāreṇa varṇānam-avedya-vedanena ca/ svakarmaṇāṃ ca tyāgena jāyante varṇa-saṁkarāḥ// saṁkīrṇa-yonayo ye tu pratilo-mānulomajāḥ/ anyonya-vyatiṣaktāśca tān pravakṣyāmyaśeṣataḥ//*) (Manu, X, 24-25).

The degraded position of the further intermixture of blood between different pratilomajā-s is expressed in Manu[84] where we come across Sairindhra, Maitreya and Mārgava, born of an Āyogavi by the Dasyu tribe, the Vaideha and a Niṣāda respectively and also their low professions. A Sairindhra is stated to be expert in hair-dressing, living the life of a slave (dāsajīvanam) and living on hunting deer etc. by nets. A Maitreya is engaged in a better vocation, he sings praises of men, while ringing the bells on boats and he is known as a kaivarta in Āryāvarta (mid-India). The Kārāvaras, born of a Niṣāda and Vaidehī live on hides (carmakāra). The Andhras and Medas, born of a Kārāvara-mother and a Niṣāda-mother respectively by a Vaideha are noted as living at the outskirt of a village, obviously as outcastes. The Āyogavī-s are also stated to be of a very low order (jātihīnā), wearing garments of the dead, and eating the rest of meals taken by others (*mṛta-vastra-bhṛtsu nāriṣu garhitān-nāśanāsu*).[85] A Caṇḍala produces in a Vaidehī a Pāṇḍusopāka living on canes; an Āniṇḍika is the product of the union between a Niṣāda and a Vaidehī and a Caṇḍāla produces in a Pukkasī a Sopāka who is full of vices and living a condemnable life, occupied with the task of an executioner[86] (*mūla-vyasana-Vṛttimān.... pāpāḥ sadā sajjana-garhitāḥ*). A Caṇḍāla again is stated to have produced in a Niṣādi an Antyāvasāyī to be engaged in a burning ground (śmaśānagocarā) and he is condemned even by all the pratilomaja-s (*vāhyānāmapi garhitaḥ*).

From the Kāmasūtra of Vātsyāyana also we learn that caste consideration was the primary factor in cases of marriage for preserving the purity of blood. Endogamy was practised with restrictions imposed on the intermixture of castes, as reflected in the Jātaka[87] (*athasya mātāpitaro samāna-jātīyaṃ kulato dārikaṃ ānayiṃsu*). While sending men for finding a bride, they were asked to choose a bride of the equal family and caste.[88] The *Āsvalāyana Gṛhyasūtra*[89] also confirms the same fact insisting on the purity of family both on the side of mother and father (*Kulam agre parīkṣeta ye mātṛtaḥ pitṛta-ś-ceti yathoktaṃ purastāt*). The Jātakas show how such caste and family restrictions on marriage were sometimes relaxed only in the higher circle of the society, as evidenced by the case of a general Ahipāraka marrying Unmadantī,[90] daughter of a merchant. Love affair was also at the root of such intercaste marriage as in the case of a king marrying Sujātā,[91] a beautiful daughter of a greengrocer selling jujubis.

We hear also of a barbar's son[92] falling in love with a Licchavi girl who had expressed his desire for her to his father and who was told that a bride of his own caste would be secured. From this we may infer that pratiloma marriage was held, though not widely in practice in the society (*aññyaṃte jāti-gottehi sadisakumārikaṃ ānesāmiti āha*). Vātsyāyana who is more concerned with the physical side of marriage is no less mindful of the other ideals of worldly gain, social status and spiritual welfare of the pair and he insists on marriage with a virgin, not given to anyone before and born of the same caste. Vātsyāyana[93] quotes the opinions of five ancient authorities on erotics who allow love with a girl of high family past her childhood and he agrees with them regarding such connection with a married woman of a higher varṇa to have been in practice, without involving the breach of Dharma. The story of a Brāhmaṇa Cārudatta marrying Vasantasenā and also of another Brāhmaṇa Sarvilaka marrying her slave Madanikā in *Mṛcchakaṭikam* and the story of a prince marrying the younger daughter of a courtesan of Campā in *Daśākumāracaritam* also confirm the recognition of such intercaste marriages in the society, as approved by Vātsyāyana, noted above.

Kauṭilya[94] also refers to some cases of intercaste marriage and mentions the mixed castes like Ambaṣṭha, Niṣāda and Ugra, termed as a-savarṇa. The offspring of a Vaiśya by a Śūdra wife has, however, been expressly designated as a Śūdra (*Śūdra eva Vaiśyasya*) and so he does not give him the status of a sajāti or sadṛśa denouncing thereby the mixture of a Śūdra blood with the blood of a higher caste. He refers to pratiloma like Āyogava, Kṣattā and Caṇḍāla and some others like Manu but he speaks highly of Sūta and Māgadha as being 'Celebrated' in the Purāṇas and quite different and of greater merit than either Brāhmaṇas or Kṣattriyas. Thus we may assume that pratiloma marriage was not so bitterly denounced in the *Arthaśāstra* as in *Manusaṃhitā* and in later Dharmaśāstras. Even the offsprings of mixed castes (antarālas) like Kukkuṭaka, Pulkasa, Vaiṇa, Kuśilava and Svapāka are allowed to have equal divisions of inheritance. From the chapter[95] on the laws of inheritance we learn that Kauṭilya sanctions intercaste marriage and prescribes inheritance even to the sons like Sūta, Māgadha, Vrātya and Rathakāra. He was also in favour of marriage within the same caste and of one with a girl of less difference of degrees in the hierarchical order; but he did not desire to deprive any issue by intercaste marriage, even a Pāraśava, i.e., a son of a Śūdra by a Brahmin.

Next let us survey the position of intercaste marriage as painted in *Yājñavalkyasmṛti*[96] which is generally placed in the Gupta period. He defines sajāti as sons born of the parents of the same Varṇa (*savarṇebhyaḥ savarṇāsu jāyante hi sajātahaḥ*) and speaks highly of them as products of 'blameless marriages' (*anindyeṣu vivāheṣu*) and as the agents of continuing the line (*santāna-vardhanāḥ*). The later Vedic period witnessed the rise of mixed castes and the jurists from Gautama onward created the different theories of cross-breeds by anuloma and pratiloma to adjust new factors of the society. Yāj. mentions six sub-castes like Mūrdhāvaṣikta, Ambaṣṭha, Niṣāda, Māhiṣya, Ugra and Karaṇa as anulomaja-s : "From a Brāhmaṇa in a Kṣattriya girl is born a Mūrdhāvaṣikta, in a Vaiśya an Ambaṣṭha and in a Śūdra a Niṣāda or Pāraśava. From a Kṣattriya in a Vaiśyā or Śūdrā respectively are born a Māhiṣya and an Ugra and from a Vaiśya in a Śūdrā is born a Karaṇa.[97] From his remark that the anulomas are sat or good, while the pratilomas are asat or bad (*asat-santa-s-tu vijñeyāḥ pratilomanulomajāḥ*),[98] we may only infer the social status of these sub-castes. Kane,[99] however thinks that anulomas are sat or good in the sense that they deserved sacraments. If so, a Niṣāda or a Pāraśava would be entitled to sacraments and thus the anulomas secured the status of their fathers. Kane[100] refers to three different views of the jurists on their issue: (i) the son of a father of any Varṇa by the mother of the next lower Varṇa would be recognised as belonging to the Varṇa of the father, (ii) the progeny of the anuloma marriage is in status lower than the father but higher than the mother and (iii) such a progeny secures the status of the mother, as held by Viṣṇu[101] and Śaṅkha quoted by Vijñāneśvara who, while commenting on Yāj.[102] endorses the last view (*Yat tu brāhmaṇena Kṣattriyāyāmutpāditaḥ Kṣattriya eva bhavati Kṣattriyeṇa Vaiśyāyām-utpādito Vaiśya eva bhavati Vaiśyena śūdrāyam-utpāditaḥ śūdra eva bhavati*). Manu outlines a new pattern of behaviour towards the wives of different castes. He shows distinctly that the wife from a lower varṇa was no better than a mistress (IX, 85-87 and 123 f). Manu's pattern was accepted by Viṣṇu D.S. (XXIV, 5-8) which states: "If he has several wives of different varṇa-s, the wife of his own varṇa enjoys the privilege of performing the religious rites, even though she is the youngest. If he has no wife of his own varṇa, or if the savarṇa-wife is absent, the wife of the next highest varṇa usually occupies the next place; but a Śūdra wife shall always be excluded from this privilege".

Kapadia has rightly answered the question why the Brahmin legislators did advocate hypergamy: (the theory of anuloma marriage) "might have helped considerably the endogamous tendency of the Brahmins, which, Ghurye has shown, found expression during their stay in the Gangetic valley. In addition it sought to fix permanently a social hierarchy in which the ascendancy of the Brahmin over the Kṣattriya was categorically asserted. The rule of anuloma and pratiloma marriages has greater significance for the caste structure of Hindu society than for the marriage pattern of the Hindus at this period in their social history. Its significance for the marriage pattern lies in the fact that the social hierarchy provides the basis, and the anuloma theory divine sanction for future hypergamy in India". (*Marriage and family in India*, pp. 104-5).

The Dharmasūtras and Dharmaśāstras frame rules for the period of impurity (aśaucha), caused by the death of relatives of different castes and thus indirectly throw light on the prevalence of intercaste marriages in the period of their composition. In cases of partition of properties, sons born of mothers belonging to different castes are said to have been entitled to their shares. Thus we learn indirectly of the possibility of intercaste marriage. A pupil is again enjoined to salute the wives of his teacher belonging to different lower castes from a distance and not to touch their feet. One could also adopt a child belonging to a different caste. Hence these evidences prove the existence of intercaste marriages.

It is interesting to note in this connection the remark of Dr. Sudhakar Chattopadhyay[103] on some names of the mixed castes, noted before, as for example, ambaṣṭha, niṣāda, māhiṣya and ugra. These are "the designations of different tribes of unaryan origin" and "they have not only entered into the Brahmanical society but have gained some status as well, as they are called 'sat'." The ambaṣṭhas lived in the western Punjab, as noted in the *Mbh.*[104] and this tribe has been located in the Geography of Ptolemy[105] in the east of the Paropanisadai. They might have belonged to the same stock as Austro-Asiatic tribes living in this region, as shown by J. Prezyluski.[106]

Gradually they migrated to the eastern regions of India, as referred to by H.C. Raychaudhuri[107] and they were Aryanised so as to be called Brāhmaṇa in the Ambaṣṭha sutta.[108] Manu[109] prescribes the profession of medicine for an Ambaṣṭha and the Vaidyas of Bengal may be accepted as descendants of Manu's Ambaṣṭhas.[110] The Niṣāda-s are noted in the *AB*[111] as evildoers (pāpakṛtaḥ) and they are so called because sin or evil sits down in him, as explained in Nirukta[112] and they are the fifth caste. Evidently they were the non-aryan tribes, mentioned as early as the Yajurveda, epics and purāṇas. The *Vāyu-purāṇa*[113] describes them as 'dark and dwarfish and living on the Vindhya. Bühler refers to another class of Niṣādas, born of pratiloma marriage, living on fisheries. The Māhiṣyas are noted as Kaivarta in Manu and later in the *Brahmavaivarta-purāṇa*. The Ugras are noted as a tribe in the Sūtrakṛtāṅga, as associated with the Bhogas, Kauravas and Aikṣvkāka-s and the Licchavis and in the Anguttara-nikāya as connected with Veśāli. The Ugra is, however, noted as anulomaja, born of a Kṣattriya in a Śūdrā in *Bodhāyana D.S.*[115] (1.9.5) [cf. Manu (X. 9). *AŚ* (iii. 7), *Yāj*. (91-92) and Anuśāsana (48.7)]. He is called a rājaputa in the Sahyādrikhaṇḍa. The Ugras are still living in the districts of Birbhum and Burdwan of West Bengal. Similarly the pratiloma subcastes like the Vaidehakas and Māgadhas were evidently non-aryan people of Bihar, Videha and Magadha.

The Rathakāra is an interesting issue. The *TB*[116] refers to the placing of the fire (agnyādhāna) by a Rathakāra in the rainy season with the mantra "*ṛbhūṇām tvā*". Jaimini[117] raises the question and concludes that the Rathakāra is the member of a caste other than the three higher Varṇa-s, called Saudhanvana, representing a caste below the Vaiśya but superior to the Śūdra. *Bodh. D.S.*[118] refers to a Rathakāra as the offspring of a Vaiśya in a Śūdrā. (*Vaiśyāt śūdrāyāṃ rathakāraḥ*). Yāj.,[119] however, mentions the Rathakāra as the progeny of the intermixture of further crossbreeds, begotten by a Māhiṣya male and a karaṇa female, i.e., a doubly mixed Anuloma (*māhiṣyena karaṇyām tu rathakāraḥ prajāyate*). Vijñāneśvara comments that this single instance is said only as a matter of illustration, as it is impossible to enumerate the various sub-castes, formed by such intermixture. (*etacca pradarśana-mātram-uktam. Saṁkīrṇa saṅkara-jātīnam-ānantyād - vaktum - aśakyatvāt*). Rathakāra was evidently an occupational caste living on the making of chariots. Manu[120] refers to Sūtas as occupied with the cares of horses and chariots (*aśva-sārathyam*), but they are noted in the *Mbh.*[121] as servants of the Brāhmaṇas and Kṣattriyas (*Brahma-Kṣattrasya vihitāḥ sūtā vai paricārakāḥ*). Manu states clearly that these mixed castes and sub-castes (*saṅkara jātaya-s-tvetāḥ pitṛ-mātṛ-pradarśitāḥ pracchannā vā prakāśā vā veditayyāḥ svakarmabhiḥ*), as described by their parents should be known by their occupations, concealed or disclosed. This statement proves that Varṇa-theory was closely associated wish the Jāti-theory, both operating simultaneously in the society.

Manu[122] refers to Madhyadeśa as the seat of ideal Brahmanical culture. The anuloma or pratiloma sub-castes or other mixed castes bearing a tribal name can not be located in this region, at least upto the period of Manu. Bodhāyana states clearly that the mixed castes live outside this region in the countries of Avantī, Aṅga, Magadha, Surāṣṭra, Dakṣiṇāpatha, Upāvṛtsindhu and Sauvīra. This belt of the unaryan tribes has been called the outer band of the Aryan group by the linguisticians. Thus we may assume that these tribal people were gradually incorporated into the Brahmanical fold under the influence of

Aryan culture and that is why the Dharmaśāstras have created the myths of anulomas and pratilomas.

Now the question may be raised if the mixed castes, as noted above, were born of regular marriages or of clandestine unions. From the above discussion it is quite clear that marriage, anuloma or pratiloma was always recognised in the society, though, of course, with a difference in degree. Anuloma was definitely preferred to pratilomas which were generally looked down upon but still sanctioned in the society, as evidenced by the recognition of the pratilomajas and by their right of inheritance. Some of the mixed castes might have been produced by clandestine unions. Uśanas[123] draws our attention to the distinction between regular and clandestine unions when he says distinctly that if a Kṣattriya marries a Brāhmaṇa girl, the issues are Sūta but if their union is clandestine, the issues are Rathakāra-s (*brāhmaṇayām kṣattriyāccauryād rathakāraḥ prakīrtitaḥ*).

Parāśara speaks of some mixed castes in the Prāyaścitta chapter, born of anuloma marriage and allows the partaking of food prepared by anuloma castes. Hence anuloma marriage was definitely sanctioned in the then society. Of course, he is silent on the marriage of a twice-born with a Śūdra girl. Bṛhaspati[124] also speaks of anuloma offsprings. However, he denies the offspring of a Śūdra by any twice-born the right of inheritance and so we may surmise that he did not approve of such marriage.

Kātyāyana[125] allows anuloma marriage but he does not approve of any Śūdra wife of a twice-born as being employed in a sacrifice. Hārīta follows suit. D.C. Sircar[126] has discussed in detail the mixed castes like Ambaṣṭhas and Kāyastha-s and shown that "the ancient Ambaṣṭhas have become Kāyasthas in Bihar and according to traditions they have formed in Bengal the communities of the Vaidyas and Māhiṣyas". We have evidence to show that Vaidyas and Kāyasthas of Bengal took to intercaste marriage between themselves. Domanadāsa, ancestor of the great Vaidya Kulīna Vamanadāsa is said to have married in the Kāyastha Pāla family in the Candraprabhā.[127] The Vaidyas and Ambaṣṭhas are noted side by side in *Uśanaḥ-saṁhitā* and in

Brahma-Vaivarta-purāṇa which gives us a mythical account of the origin of the Vaidyas. D.C. Sircar draws our attention to the fact that "the Bengal Vaidyas were regarded as śūdra by Vāchaspati Miśra, Raghunandana and Kulapañjikāras".[128] Bharata Mallika of the 17th cent. did not claim brahminhood for his community, as is done by many a Vaidya at present; but he tried to whitewash the stigma of Śūdratva from his community. Rāja Rājvallabha of the 18th cent. claimed for the Vaidyas the status of a Vaiśya and introduced the system of taking the cognomen 'gupta' for the purpose. Later on when the census system was introduced, the Vaiśyas claimed the social status of a Brāhmaṇa and began to use Śarman instead of 'gupta'. It is interesting to note that Ballālasena who is known to have introduced 'Kulīnism' among the Brāhmaṇas, Kāyasthas and Vaidyas and who claims to have been a vaidya king is born of a Brāhma Kṣattriya family, i.e. a Kṣattriya family having an admixture of brāhmaṇa-blood and hailing from the Kannaḍa-speaking area of the Deccan. Sircar also fails to accept the scheme of Manu literally regarding the mixed castes: "Of more than fifty names of the so-called mixed or degraded castes, the Malla, Magadha, Ābhira, Andhra, Āvantya, Kāruṣa, Khasa, Kirāta, Śaka, Pauṇḍra, Ambaṣṭha, Kāmboja, Pahlava, Pāraśava, Darada, Drāviḍa, Vātadhāna, Sairindhra, Coḍa or Oḍra, Veṇa, Yavana, Cīna, Sāttvata, Meda, Niṣāda etc. are known to have been tribes or communities from the lists furnished by the epics, purāṇas, works like Bṛhatsaṁhitā and other sources. The inclusion of such well-known names as the Yavana (Greek), Śaka (Scythian) etc. in the list of degraded kṣattriyas and the Ābhira, Andhra, Ambaṣṭha etc. in that of the mixed castes makes the spirit of the arbitrary scheme very clear".[129]

Romila Thapar's[130] remark on the mixed castes also deserves our attention: "In a standard Dharmaśāstra such as that of Manu the mixed castes were occasionally occupational groups but generally those tribes which obviously were not easily assimilated into Aryan society. What is interesting is that these tribal names continued to occur with separate identities right upto the medieval period. Thus we are told that a Brāhmaṇa marrying a Vaiśya woman produces children who are categorised as the Ambaṣṭha: the later purāṇas refer to the Ambaṣṭha tribe as deriving its origin from the Ānava Kṣattriyas and the tribal identity remains..... clearly the tribes which were not assimilated had to be given a ritual status in the system and thus the theory of mixed castes was worked out". It is interesting to note that ritual status gave eminence to a particular caste in the society, specially to those who were known as dvija, twice-born, i.e., the upper three castes. The Yavanas and Śakas who came to India and settled here, are regarded as aniravasita (pure) śūdra but they are enlisted by Manu as 'degraded Kṣattriyas'. The Kāyasthas who served as scribes, as known from Gupta records were gradually evolved into a caste and were given a low ritual status; and the myth was invented to show their origin from the intermixture of the Brāhmaṇas and Śūdras.

The Una Pillar inscription[131] of Avantivarman II (899 A.D.) refers to a Cālukya feudatory of the Pratihāra king taking pride in "freeing the earth from the Hūṇa peoples". Another record of almost the same period, Ātpur ins.[132] of Śaktikumāra speaks of a Guhila king of the Udaipur region marrying the daughter of a Hūna king. But the founder of the Guhila dynasty claims to be a Brāhmaṇa. Thus intercaste or interracial marriage broke the kinship barrier and even the foreign rulers were elevated to the status of the Āryas in the society for all practical purposes.

Let us consider some other mixed castes, referred to in the Dharma literature as the names of progeny of intercaste-married couples:

Antyāvasāyin: *Vas. D.S.*[133] mentions this Varṇa as the offspring of a Śūdra from a Vaiśya woman, but Manu[134] takes it as the issue of a Caṇḍāla male in a Niṣāda female. This caste is represented by Ḍom-s at present.

Ābhīra: According to Manu[135] an Ābhīra is the child of a union of a Brāhmaṇa with an Ambaṣṭha woman. He is noted as a dasyu or a mleccha in the *Mbh.*[136] and as a śūdra.[137] The

Mahābhāṣya[138] mentions this as a caste distinct from the śūdras (*ābhīrā jātyantarāṇi*). According to Daṇḍin[139] an Ābhīra speaks in apabhraṃśa dialect. They were obviously foreigners, settled first in N.W. part of India and next moving to different regions like Mathurā, Marubhūmi, Bharukaccha, and Saurāṣṭra. They were gradually absorbed in the Hindu society, as reflected in the myths of the smṛtis, epics and purāṇas. The Daulatpur ins. of Ābhīra Iśvaradeva (Śaka year 254) refers to the king as grandson of Jyaitrika of Saudaskara gotra who gave donation to Dyutisvāmin of Āryagotra. The region of Ābhīra may be equated with Abhiria, mentioned in the Periplus and in the Geography of Ptolemy. Their social status is referred to in the Kāśikā as being incorporated into the frame work of the caste system as Mahāśūdras. The gotras, noted in the Daulatpur ins. (Saudaskara and Ārya) indicate the Brahmin origin of the king and also the race of the donee. Benveniste suggests the derivation of Ārya from 'aris' for an individual of that part of the tribe into which he or she might lawfully marry. Āryas might be descendants of Aris, the offspring of legitimate marriage unions. The Āryagotra suggests the name of the race but at the same time it is an interesting ancestral brahmin name, evidently distinct from those Ābhīras who were taken as Vrātyas. The gotra Saudaskarasa indicates that the Ābhīras had their ethnic names. This and another gotra 'Harivobaka' in the Mewasa ins.[140] suggest their Iranian origin. The Nasik cave (No. 15) ins.[141] refers to king Iśvarasena, a son of Ābhīra Śivadatta and Māṭharī, that means, a progeny of intercaste marriage.

Kukkuṭa : a pratiloma caste, according to *Bodhāyana D.S.*,[142] noted as the child of a Śudra in a Niṣādi in the same source[143] and even as that of a Vaiśya in a Niṣādī.[144] Manu[145] follows Bodhāyana but Kauṭilya[146] speaks of him as the product of an Ugra male in a Niṣādī.

Kuśilava : The Kṛtyakalpataru quotes from Bodhāyana a passage showing that he is the child of an Ambaṣṭha from a Vaidehaka woman. Kauṭilya[147] states the reverse of this fact, that is, he is the offspring of a Vaidehaka from an Ambaṣṭha female.

Caṇḍāla: He is noted in the *Chāndogya upa*.[148] as the lowest in the social scale. The Dharma literature[149] mentions him as pratilomaja, born of a śūdra from a brāhmaṇī. Mataṅga is described as a Caṇḍāla in the Anuśāsana,[150] being born of a barber in a brāhmaṇī. Svapāka, Domba and Caṇḍāla are spoken of as belonging to the same category by Parāśara, quoted by Aparārka.

Takṣan: He is regarded as an unholy person (amedhya) in the *ŚB*.[151] Uśanas (43) describes him as the child of a brāhmanī from a sūchaka, thus a pratilomaja.

Sūta and Rathakāra: These two are mentioned in the *AV*., Yāj, and Brāhmaṇas as a caste on the basis of their occupations. Sūta is noted as a pratilomaja in the smṛtis of Gautama (IV. 15), *Bodh. D.S.* (1, 9, 9) Manu (X. II) and Viṣṇu (16, 6), as a child of a Kṣattriya in a Brāhmaṇī. Rathakāra is again described in *Bodh. D.S.*[152] as the offspring of a Vaiśya in a Śūdrā; but as a doubly mixed caste in Yāj. (1.95).

Sairindhra: Manu[153] speaks of this as the offspring of a dasyu from an āyogava woman, occupied with combing the hair of men and women and engaged in menial works. The *Mbh*.[154] refers to Draupadī disguised as a sairindhrī and to Damayantī as serving the mother of a Cedi king.

R.C. Majumdar[155] has pointed out that "while the different castes, mentioned in the Smṛtis, undoubtedly represent actual state of things, not the least historical value can be attached to the puerile fiction of their derivation from specified union of males and females belonging to different varṇas. Yet .... there can be hardly any doubt that the people generally believed in this theory of mixed castes and it exercised a great influence in determining the status of the different castes and subcastes in the society".

LITERARY AND EPIGRAPHIC EVIDENCES

We hear of a matrimonial alliance between Seleucus and Candragupta Maurya.[156] George Macdonald remarks: "Invader and invaded, we are told, concluded an alliance and sealed it by a further compact which Appian (Syr. 55) calls a 'Kedos' and Strabo,[157] an epigamia intermarriage". So there is no doubt about matrimonial alliance between two royal families. It is a well-known fact that the foreigners were gradually Indianised and placed in the social organisation of this country; e.g. Gautama regards the Yavanas (Greeks) as the offspring of a Kṣattriya male and a Śūdra female. We have noted that Manu[158] regards the Kāmboja-s, Yavanas, Śakas etc. as degraded Kṣattriyas but the Śakas and Yavanas are recognised as pure (aniravasita) Śūdras in the *Mahābhāṣya*. The non-aryan peoples like the Pauṇḍrakas, Coḍas, Drāviḍas, Kirātas, Daradas, and Khasas are also treated as degraded Kṣattriyas in Manusmṛti. Candragupta Maurya belonged apparently to the Moriya clan of the Himalayan Mangoloids living in the Pippalīvana areas about the Terai of Nepal. They are called Vṛṣala-s or śudras by some orthodox writers (cf. Mudrārākṣasa), but they claimed to be pure Kṣattriyas, (Cf, Divyāvadāna). Hence we may accept the prevalence of not only intercaste but also interracial marriage in ancient India. It is interesting to add that some of the Rajput Kṣattriya clans were of foreign or non-aryan origin, the Solankis and Rāṭhods were of Karṇāta region and the Paṇidhāras were foreigners of the Hūna-Gurjara stock.[159] The term 'Yavana' in the earlier inscriptions of India means a Greek and not a Persian, as held by some scholars. The process of Indianisation of the Greeks and other foreigners has been treated in my "Early Brāhmī Records in India".[161] The very name of Dinika suggests that he was a foreigner, but the name of his son Usabhadāta (Ṛṣabhadatta) points to his Indianisation. He was the son-in-law of Kṣaharāta Nahapāna whose daughter bore the Hindu name of Dakṣamitrā (*E.I.*, VIII, p. 81). The names of some Yavanas of Dhenukakaṭa like Dhamma, Indrāgnidatta etc., found in the inscription of Karle (*E.I.*, VII, No. 10 and VIII, No. 18) also speak of such Indianisation of foreigners. The process of assimilation became complete in the 2nd and 3rd centuries A.D. when the orthodox kings of the Sātavahana and Ikṣvāku dynasties married the girls of the Kṣattrapas ruling in Western India, as evidenced by the Kanheri ins.[162] which mentions "the queen of Vāsiṣṭhiputra Siri Sātakarṇi "to be born of the race of the "Kardamaka" kings, daughter of Mahākṣattrapa". Rudra Bhaṭṭārikā, chief queen of Vīrapuruṣadatta was the daughter of the Śaka king of Ujjayinī, probably Rudrasena I (200-244 A.D.) or Rudrasena II[163] (254-74 A.D.). From the Mathura ins.[164] of the year 20 we learn of Mitrā, daughter of a jeweller but daughter-in-law of a blacksmith (Lohakāra), another evidence of intercaste marriage in the society of the Kushāṇa period. From the Nasik ins.[165] also we find that Usavadāta, a Śaka married a Hindu or Buddhist wife Sanghamitrā.

The Junagarh ins.[166] of 150 A.D. describes the Kārdamaka Śaka Mahākṣattrapa Rudradāman I as one who received as his share many garlands in the svayaṁvaras of princesses (*narendra-kanyā-svayaṁvarāneka-mālyaprapta-dāmanaḥ*). Svayaṁvara was a typical Kṣattriya custom and thus the Śaka king Rudradāman indirectly claims to have married many Kṣattriya girls. Besides, this ins. also refers to the close connection between Śaka Rudradāman and king Sātakarṇi of Dakṣiṇāpatha, obviously Gautamīputra Sātakarṇi who claims to have been "the unique Brāhmaṇa". The Sātavāhanas were Dravidians but claimed the status of the Brāhmaṇa apparently owing to a little Brāhamṇa blood in their veins.[167]

The Ikṣvāku king Ehuvula Sāntamūla (285-335 A.D.), son of Vīrapuruṣadatta married Varmabhaṭā, daughter of the Mahākṣattrapa of the Bṛhatphalāyana gotra undoubltedly to be identified with a Śaka king of Western India.[168] That Varmabhaṭā belonged to the Śaka house of Western India is proved by her father's designation Mahākṣattrapa and also by her representation on the Chāyāstambha (figure-bearing memorial pillar), raised for her which shows her in a foreign lady's dress (udīcya-veśa).

A seal of Mahādevī Prabhudāmā, daughter of Mahākṣattrapa Rudrasinha I and sister of Rudrasena I has been unearthed from Vaiśālī.[169] She seems to have been married with a king of the locality. Another Mahārāja Rudradāma or Rudradāmaśrī of the Mirzapur district (U.P.) of the 3rd cent. A.D. was probably married to a ruler of the Mirzapur region.[170]

Candragupta II, married Kuveranāgā of the Nāga family, evidently non-aryan and his daughter Prabhāvatīgupta was married with the Brahmin king Rudrasena II of the Vākāṭaka family.[171]

Kākusthavarman of the Kadamba family having the status originally of a Brāhamaṇa but later on of a Kṣattriya gave one of his daughters in marriage to a Gupta King.[172]

The account of Yuan Chwang[173] reports that the daughter of Harṣa of Thaneswar belonging to Vaiśya family married a Kṣattriya king of Valabhi.

The matrimonial alliance between the Palas of Bengal and the Karṇāṭa-Dravidian Rāṣṭrakūṭas of the Deccan[174] and between the Gāhaḍavāla king Govindacandra and the Karṇāṭa-Chikkora (Dravidian princess Kumāradevī)[175] bespeak the prevalence of intercaste marriage even among the ruling families of different parts of ancient India. Raṇṇādevī, queen of Dharmapāla was the daughter of a Rāṣṭrakūṭa chief named Parabala, Bhāgyadevī, daughter of Rāṣṭrakūṭa chief Tuṅga was the queen of king Rājyapāla and the king Vigrahapāla - III married the sister of Rāṣṭrakūṭa Mathana who ruled over Aṅga under the Pālas. Mathana's daughter Śaṅkarādevī was married to the chief Devarakṣita of the Chikkora family of Pīṭhi (Bodhgayā).

A Jodhpur ins.[176] of the feudatory Pratihāra family records that a brāhmaṇa named Harichandra and surnamed Rohilladdhi had two wives, one brāhmaṇa and the other a kṣattriya woman and their children were called Brāhmaṇa-pratihāra-s and Kṣattriya-pratihāra-s in accordance with the caste of their mothers. It is another instance of intercaste marriage. The Smṛtis, we have already noticed, allow such anuloma marriage and the progeny is relegated to a class of mixed castes and has nowhere been called a Kṣattriya. But here we come across the term 'Kṣattriya-pratihāra'. Elsewhere Soma is said to have married two such wives, a Brāhmaṇa and a Kṣattriya in the Ghaṭotkaca inscription[177] (5th cent. A.D.) of Yaśodharman and Viṣṇuvardhana:

"Soma-s-tataḥ soma ivāparo' bhūt sa brāhmaṇaḥ Kṣattriya-Vaṃśa-jāsu/ śruti-smṛtibhyāṃ vihitārthakārī dvayīṣu bhāryāsu mano dadhāra//".

The Tippera C.P. ins.[178] of Lokanātha (*c.* 650 A.D.) states that Lokanātha's ancestors were of Bharadwāja gotra and that his maternal grandfather Keśava was a Pārāśava and that Keśava's father Vīra was a Brahmin.

The Ātpur ins. of Śaktikumāra (977 A.D.) states that Guhadatta, founder of the Guhila dynasty was a Brahmin but his descendant Bhartṛpaṭṭa married a Rāṣṭrakūṭa princess. Virūpadevī[179] daughter of Bukka I, king of Vijayanagara (1268-98 A.D.) was married with a brāhmaṇa, named Brahma or Bomaṇṇa[180] Woḍeyar, governor of the Āraga province (*E.I.*, vol. XV, p. 12).

Next we come across literary evidences. The *Mbh.* refers to the story of Kāyavya, son of a Niṣādī by a Kṣattriya who, though a dasyu, attained to perfection (siddhi) by virtue of his merits he had acquired by fulfilling varṇāśrama-dharma and respectful service to his parents. This legend shows that intercaste marriage was no bar to one's spiritual rise. D.R. Bhandarkar[181] also finds in a verse of the *Mbh.*[182] *tato brāhmaṇatām jāto Viśvāmitro mahātapāḥ/ Kṣattriya so'pyatha tathā brahma-vaṃśyasya kārakaḥ/ /* "a clear instance of the fusion of the brāhmaṇa and Kṣattriya blood". Ajāmiḍha[183] was a kṣattriya but from him sprang Kāṇvāyana brāhmaṇa-s. The discussion of various mixed castes like Atiratha, Ambaṣṭha, Ugra, Vaidehaka, Śvapāka, Pukkaśa, Niṣāda, Sūta, Māgadha, Madranābha, Āhiṇḍaka, Carmakāra, Saupāka and others in the Śāntiparvan[184] throws welcome light on the system of intercaste marriage in the period concerned.

Ghurye[185] speaks of Sumitrā as daughter of a śūdra, though he has not substantiated it with any evidence. But her sons by Daśaratha were recognised as full-fleged kṣattriyas. Śravaṇa-kumāra, son of Andhamuni whom Daśaratha had killed was the son of a śūdra mother and vaiśya-father.[186] However, he had matted hair on his head and barkgarment and led the life of a hermit. Daśaratha was shocked at his death. The blind hermit told Daśaratha that one who would strike such a hermit (taponiṣṭha and brahmavādin) with a missile, would have his head divided into seven parts.[187] Daśaratha, however, did this offence unknowingly and so he was freed from the sin of Brahmin-murder (brahma-hatyā). From this it is evident that Daśaratha would have incurred such sin of brahma-hatyā, if he had knowingly killed the hermit boy, son of a Vaiśya father by a śūdra wife.

The Buddhist records also throw light on intercaste marriage. The Ambaṭṭha sutta[188] of the *Dīgha-nikāya* gives us a dialogue between Buddha and Ambaṣṭha. Ambaṣṭha admits that his ancestor Kanha was the son of Diśa, a slave of king Okkaka (Ikṣvāku) from whom the Śākyas traced their descent. This Kanha married a daughter of the king Okkaka. Gautama Buddha says that the son of a Kṣattriya by a Brāhmaṇī would be respected by the Brahmins but would not receive the consecration ceremony of a Kṣattrīya, because, "he is not of pure descent on the mother's side", similar answers came from Ambaṭṭha when he was asked about a son born of a brāhmaṇa in a Kṣattriya. Buddha concludes the superiority of the Brahmins to the Kṣattriyas. However, this dialogue presents a faithful picture of social life allowing intercaste-marriage between a brahmin youth or maiden and a kṣattriya maiden or youth: and there is no reason to the contrary, the interdict against intercaste marriage should be traced not to Brāhmaṇa-narrowness but to Kṣattriya-pride.

Next we come across Śārdulakarṇa Avadāna (No. 33) of Divyāvadāna. Buddha was at Anāthapiṇḍada's garden at Jetavana at Śrāvastī. Ānanda went to Śrāvastī to beg alms. After taking his food he went to a well where he saw Prakṛti, a caṇḍāla girl drawing water and quenched his thirst by water she offered. Prakṛti was charmed with Ānanda and fell in love and expressed her desire to her mother, but the mother disagreed out of fear from the king Prasenajit. However, Prakṛti approached the Lord Buddha praying for the hand of Ānanda and told him the consent of her parents. She was at last taken in as a nun of the Buddhist order. When Prasenajit asked Buddha the reason behind this initiation of a Caṇḍāla girl, Buddha explained with the life-history in her previous birth. Once there lived Triśanku, a king of Caṇḍālas on the Ganges, who was again a Brahmin in his previous birth, well-versed in the Vedas. Triśanku remembered the Vedic knowledge in the present life and imparted it to his son named Śārdulakarṇa. Puskarasari, a learned Brahmin had a daughter called Prakṛti. Triśanku wanted the hand of Prakṛti for his son. Puskarasari was highly enraged and reminded Triśanku that none should marry out of his own caste. Triśanku replied that there was no real difference between a Brāhmaṇa and other castes. Puskarasari explained the law of intercaste marriage and origin of four varṇas from Brahma. Triśanku's reply is more interesting, as it points out that castes are like dust-balls made by little girls at play and named curd, meat, ghee etc. and concludes that men belong to one caste. Puskarasari agreed to give his daughter Prakṛti to Śārdulakarṇa. Triśanku refers to two well-known Brāhmaṇa sages of mixed parentage, Dvaipāyana, born of Niṣādi Kālī and Rāma (Paraśurāma), born of a Kṣattriya mother, Reṇukā.

Another evidence named Pāṃśu-pradānāvadāna (No. 26 of Dviyāvadāna) may be mentioned here. During the rule of Bindusāra at Pāṭaliputra lived a Brahmin at Campa who was blessed with a fine daughter about whom astrologers predicted that she would be married to a king and give birth to two sons, one overlord of the earth and the other a monk. She was offered to Bindusāra and placed in his harem. She was assigned the duty of a barber by her cowives. However, she was at last treated as the wife and became the mother of Aśoka and Vītāśoka. All these Buddhist tales testify to the prevalence of intercaste marriage, at least to a limited extent in the society.

Intercaste marriage is also referred to in Kālidāsa's work, *Mālavikāgnimitra* describing Agnimitra, a Brahmin by caste as marrying Mālavikā, a Kṣattriya princess. The term Varṇāvaraḥ meaning 'born of a lower caste', is used in the *Mālavikāgnimitram* (p. 9). Vīrasena, a general and half-brother of queen Dhāriṇī is noted as born of a step-mother of a lower caste in this story. Bāṇa[189] mentions in *Harṣacaritam* that he had two Pāraśava brothers called Candrasena and Maitrasena. Daṇḍin paints in *Daśakumāracaritam* the picture of the institution of four castes. Yuan Chwang[190] also corroborates the same fact of the division of the society into four castes, along with their respective occupations, having their matrimonial alliances within the caste. But Daṇḍin refers to deviations from the rigid law of castes, as in *Daśakumāracarita.*[191] Saunama, a Brahmin is noted as marrying the princess of the Kośala king and a courtesan maid. (vide also. ed. M.R. Kavi (Madras), 1924, *Avantīsundarī-Kathā*, IV, 174). Bhāsa, an earlier dramatist mentions Brahmin Cārudatta's marriage with Vasantasenā, a courtesan and also similar union between Śarvilaka, the Brahmin and her slave. The Brahmins had no bar in marrying girls of other castes and even courtesans.[192] In DKC[193] and in ASK[194] we find the mention of Mūladeva having a courtesan wife and of the Brahmin Śūdraka's love for Raṅgapatāka an actress. It is interesting to note that Daṇḍin refers to not only a Brāhmaṇa's love for a harlot but also to an ascetic's yearning for her as in Marīci's fondness for Kāmamañjarī.[196] Elsewhere[197] we find the instance of intercaste marriage which might have prevailed among people of higher circle like kings and rich traders who had to make long trips and who sometimes settled at distant places.

Gautama[198] speaks of this change by intercaste marriage. (*Varṇāntara-gamanam-utkarṣāpakarṣābhyāṃ saptame pañcame vā ācāryaḥ sṛṣṭyantara-jātānām ca*). If a bride marries the male of a higher varṇa in each generation, by such anuloma marriage their offspring rises to the higher Varṇa in the seventh generation and likewise, if a bride marries a male of a lower varṇa, by such pratiloma marriage in each generation, their issue falls to the lower varṇa in the fifth generation. Suppose that a Brāhmaṇa marries a Kṣattriya girl, the daughter born of such union is a Savarṇa and if this daughter is married with a Brāhmaṇa and a daughter is again born and if she is again married with a Brāhmaṇa, and if this process goes on, then in the seventh generation, the child is recognised as a Brāhmaṇa. On the contrary, if the son of a Savarṇa, noted above, marries a Kṣattriya girl and gives birth to a son, who in turn marries a Kṣattriya girl and gets a son, then by this process being continued, the child of the fifth generation would be regarded a Kṣattriya. These rules are applicable to the members of other Varṇa-s as well. A Savarṇa male may marry a Savarṇa girl for generations together, and if so, the issue becomes a Savarṇa in the seventh generation or he may marry an Ambaṣṭha girl for generations together, and if so, the progeny becomes an Ambaṣṭha in the fifth generation.[199]

Āpastamba[200] says that one's caste may be changed in the next birth by means of his action in the present one: "In successive births men of the lower castes are born in the next higher one, if they have fulfilled their duties. In successive births men of the higher castes are born in the next lower ones, if they neglect their duties" (*dharma-caryayā jaghanyo varṇaḥ pūrvaṃ pūrvaṃ varṇam-āpadyate jātiparivṛttau adharma-caryayā purva-varṇo jaghanyaṃ varṇam-āpadyate jātiparivṛttau.*). Bodhāyana[201] frames a unique law: "*Niṣādena niṣādyām-āpañcamāt jāto'pahanti śūdratāṃ tam-upanayet - ṣaṣṭhaṃ yājayet*", which means, "If a Niṣāda, son of a Brāhmaṇa from his Śūdra wife, marries a Niṣādī and if this process continues, then in the fifth generation, he becomes free from the taint of-Śūdrahood. He may have the right of upanayana and Vedic sacrifices". Here we find Bodhāyana, unlike other jurists, to be liberal enough to raise the progeny of a Niṣāda and a Niṣādī in the fifth generation to the status of a dvija and to extend the right of upanayana and Vedic sacrifice. According to Manu,[202] if a Pāraśava daughter marries a Brāhmaṇa and her daughter again marries a Brāhmaṇa and if this process goes on continuously, "then in the seventh generation the child would be recognised as brāhmaṇa". Likewise, if a Pāraśava daughter marries a Śūdra and if their daughter again marries a Śūdra and if this process goes on continuously, then in the seventh generation the child would be regarded as a Śūdra. Manu frames rules for such rise and fall in cases of other Varṇas. According to Medhātithi and Kullūka, however, Manu means that the daughter of a Brāhmaṇa by a Vaiśya wife gains by such anuloma marriage rise to the status of a Brāhmaṇa in the fifth generation and similar connection of the son of a Brāhmaṇa by a Vaiśya leads to the fall of the caste, i.e. to the status of a Vaiśya.[203]

Yāj.[204] refers to such rise and fall of castes: "*Jātyutkarṣo yuge jñeyaḥ saptame pañcame' pi vā/vatyaye Karmaṇāṃ sāmyaṃ pūrvavaccādharottaram*" - the rise in caste is to be understood in the seventh or even in the fifth birth, by confusion of professions (comes) equality. Adhara (lower) and uttara (higher) as in the previous cases, noted before, Vijñaneśvara comments on it: "The Mūrdhāvaṣikta and other girls of (mixed) castes are raised to the status of a Brāhmaṇa and other high castes in the seventh or even fifth generation. 'Api' in the text indicates that it may be applied also in the sixth generation. This alternative is again restricted, as follows. If a Brāhmaṇa marries a Śūdra woman and gets a daughter, she is called a Niṣādī, if she again marries a Brāhmaṇa and gets a daughter who in turn marries a Brāhmaṇa and if this process continues, the sixth daughter produces the seventh child who is regarded as a Brāhmaṇa. Similarly, an Ambaṣṭha is born of a Brāhmaṇa by a Vaiśya mother. If she again marries a Brāhmaṇa and gets a daughter, thus by continuous marriage with a Brāhmaṇa the child of the fifth descent becomes a Brāhmaṇa. The Mūrdhāvaṣikta also by this process of the fourth generation produces a Brāhmaṇa fifth in descent. In this way an Ugra and Māhiṣya girl by marriage with a Kṣattriya gets a Kṣattriya child in the sixth and fifth generation respectively. A karaṇī, married with a Vaiśya following the same process for four generations, gets a Vaiśya child, fifth in descent. From this commentary we learn that the higher the position of the father and the mother, the lesser would be the number of generations. From the remark "such is to be understood in other cases also" (*evam-anyatrāpi ūhanīyam*). We may infer that such a rule would be applicable in case of the first three varṇa-s also, as expressly mentioned in the commentary of Viśvarupa known as *Bālakrīḍā*: *jātyutkarṣaḥ varṇotkarṣaḥ Kṣattriyasyāpi brāhmaṇya-prāptiḥ*.

It is interesting to note that Yāj., speaks of the rise and fall of castes not only by marriage but also due to avocations. He[205] has allocated particular professions to different castes but in times of emergency one may take to avocations of other varṇas. Gautama[206] and *Vasiṣṭha D.S.*[207] ordain that in times of emergency one is entitled to the avocation of the immediately lower varṇa (*anantarāṃ yavīyasīm*); but on the expiry of such emergency one should revert to one's original occupation. By *'vyatyaye karmaṇāṃ sāmyam'* Yāj. means to say that when a member of a higher caste follows the profession of a lower caste, then in the 5th or 7th generation the progeny gets the caste according to the profession he follows. A Brāhmaṇa may live by the profession of a Kṣattriya, a Vaiśya or even of a Śūdra if needed, for the sake of life. Similarly the members of other castes may also accept the professions of other castes. But even after the end of emergency if a Brāhmaṇa does not leave the profession of the lowest Śūdra caste, then he is degraded to the lowest caste in the seventh generation, if a Brahmin does not leave the profession of the Vaiśya, and he gets a son who also does not leave the Vaiśya's profession and if this continues, then the son becomes a Vaiśya in the 6th descent. A Brāhmaṇa produces a kṣattriya in the 5th generation, if he and his sons live by the profession of a Kṣattriya. A Kṣattriya also, by the profession of a Śūdra produces a Śūdra in the 6th generation; and by the profession of a Vaiśya, produces a Vaiśya in the 5th generation. A Vaiśya also, by the profession of a Śūdra becomes, by way of sons, a Śūdra in the 5th generation. By *'adharottaram'* Vijñāneśvara means the intermixture of pure castes with high breeds and double high breeds, as shown in the case of a Rathakāra (*māhiṣyeṇa karaṇyāṃ tu rathakāraḥ prajāyate*), an example of *saṃkīrṇa saṅkara-jātāḥ*. It is interesting to remember that a son, born of intercaste marriage gets the caste of the father, seed of the patriarchal society of the Aryans. Women were predominant in the matriarchal society. Gradually daughter's or wife's predominance was established in the Aryan society. Now-a-days Nāmbudri Brahmins of Malabar leads a family life with the girls of Nāyar community and this sort of marriage is called a mere 'relation' and not marriage and the son so produced is known as Nāyar. This system still prevails where woman is more predominant. In the *Harivaṁśa* the text:[208] *mātā bhastrā pituḥ putro yena jātaḥ sa eva saḥ*, also speaks of the superiority of the seed (i.e., father) and ordains that the son belongs to the father. But elsewhere the *Mbh.*[209] (*bhāryā-s-catasro viprasya dvayo-r-ātmā prajāyate/ ānupūrvyāddvayor-hīnau mātṛ-jātyau prasūyataḥ*) shows that generally the progeny of parents of different castes were known by the caste of the mother. It has already been noted that Manu[210] prefers savarṇa-vivāha to a-savarṇa-vivāha but admits the latter prevailing in the society. He has prescribed different modes of marriage by marrying girls of different castes in intercaste marriage. Vyāsa, however, says that sons, born of a-savarṇa girls - are not inferior to those, born of savarṇa-girls. The wife of the same caste was entitled to perform sacrifices with her husband but Kātyāyana[211] says that even the wife of the different caste was also entitled to do so. Viṣṇu[212] enjoins that next to savarṇa-wife, wives of other castes are entitled to do so in order of castes but except the Śūdra wife (26.4). Manu[213] says that this rule did not hold good always, as in cases like Vasiṣṭha marrying Akṣamālā of the lowest caste and sage Mandapāla marrying tiryak-girl Śāraṅgī (*Akṣamālā Vasiṣṭhena Saṁyuktādhama-yonijā/ śāraṅgī Mandapālena jagāmā bhyarhanīyatām// etāścānyāśca loke' smin apakṛṣṭa-prasūtayaḥ/ utkarṣaṃ yoṣitaḥ prāptāḥ svaiḥ svai-r-bhartṛ-guṇaiḥ śubhaiḥ//*). The jurists enjoin the different modes of sacraments like 'Jāta karma' for the child, born of both savarṇā and a-savarṇā.[214] However, they became less interested in subsequent days in children of a-savarṇa-wife, as evidenced by laws of inheritance. Viṣṇu[215] says that if a Brāhmaṇa has four wives of four castes, his property will be divided into ten, four shares to the son of a Brāhmaṇi, three to that of a Kṣattriyā, two to that of a Vaiśyā and one only to that of a Śūdrā. Manu[216] also confirms it. He[217] says that the son of a Śūdrā by any of three higher castes would not inherit the paternal property but whatever is given to a son by a Śūdra wife by the father, would go to the Śūdrāputra. (*brāhmaṇa-Kṣattriya-viśām śūdrāputro na-rikthabhāk/ yad-evāsya pitā dadyāt-tad-evāsya dhanam bhavet//*). The Mitākṣarā,[218] however, states that the above text of Manu

(IX. 155) applies only where the son has already got some property from his father (*tadapi jīvatā pitrā yadi śūdrāputrāya kimapi pradattaṃ syāt-tada-viṣayam*). The Mayūkha states that the above rule applies to the son of a Śūdrā, not married to the person of a higher caste but only a mistress. Kauṭilya[219] says that the Pāraśava son gets one-eighth of his father's property.

The sons of pratiloma union are, according to Gautama[220] and *Viṣṇu D.S.*[221] to be dealt with like the sons of a Brāhmaṇa from the Śūdra woman. That means they would be entitled to maintenance from their father, though the pratiloma union are condemned in the society (*Śūdrāputravat pratilomā-s-tu* and *pratilomāsu strīṣu cotpannāś cābhāginaḥ*).

The child, born of the intercaste marriage came to be known by the caste of his mother by the 10th cent. A.D., as evidenced by the remark of Alberuni[222] (1020 A.D.): "The child belongs to the caste of the mother and not to that of the father. Thus for instance, if the wife of a brāhmaṇa is a brāhmaṇa her child is also a brāhmaṇa; if she is a śūdrā, her child is also a śūdra". But the reverse we come across in *Rājataraṅginī*[223] where Candrāpīḍa and Lalitāditya were the issues of the King Pratāpāditya by a divorcee, who was formerly a wife of a trader of Rahtaka. Elsewhere[224] the mother of Śaṅkaravarman, king of Kashmīra was born in the family of low caste spirit-distiller. Śaṅkaravarman himself married an untouchable Ḍomba woman[225] and made her his chief queen.

Rājaśekhara, the poet-laureate of the Gurjara-pratihāra king married a cultured Kṣattriya lady in 860 A.D.

In *Kathāsaritsāgara* of Somadeva (1063-1080) we learn of a father asking his daughter as to which of the suitors belonging to four castes she approved[226] (*eṣāṃ caturṇāṃ varṇāṇāṃ putri ko' bhimata-s-tava*). When the Brāhmaṇa Aśokadatta was married to a princess, their union was highly spoken of, like that of learning with modesty[227] (*tayostu so'bhūd-rājanya-putri-viprendra-putrayoḥ/saṅgamo' nyonyaśobhāyai vidya-vinayayo-r-iva*). In the history of Kashmir Bālāditya, king of Gonanda dynasty is known to have given his daughter in marriage to a Kāyastha. The famous lady Diddā, daughter of the Lohara king (a Khas chief) was married to a Kṣattriya Kṣemagupta;[228] and she issued a joint coinage with her husband which is supported by coin legend.[229] Kalhaṇa, a Brāhmaṇa historian of the 12th cent. A.D. records the marriage of a sister of king Saṁgrāmarāja (1003-1028 A.D.) with a Brahmin youth. He is shocked at this marriage and he regrets that the king has brought his family into disgrace by such intercaste marriage[230] (*Paryaptaṃ tasya bhīrtutvaṃ kiyad-anyat prakāśyatām/asamair-r-yauna-saṁbhadhai-s-cakṣame yaśasaḥ Kṣatim*).

In earlier days the dead bodies of Brāhmaṇas and others could be carried to the burning ground by the Śūdra servants but in the subsequent period the Śūdra could not touch the dead bodies of the higher castes. Viṣṇu[231] states that the son's duty was to carry the dead bodies of his parents to the burning ground, but a śūdrāputra (son by a Śūdra woman) could not carry the dead body of his Brahmin father. Viṣṇu,[232] Uśanas[233] and Śañkha[234] prescribe the period of impurity due to other sons on the death of children by a-savarṇa wives. The higher three castes were to observe the purity of impurity for 10 days, because the Kṣattriyas and Vaiśyas were servants of the Brāhmaṇas and Kṣattriyas respectively and because their religious duties would go on unhampered for the period concerned.[235]

By the way, it deserves mention that intercaste marriage was allowed at least down to the 10th cent. A.D., when the members of different castes followed almost the same standard of cultural life. They were all non-vegetarians and even the Brāhmaṇas used to take meat, as least as prasāda, due share as a blissful gift when they performed the Vedic sacrifices. But after the 10th cent. things changed under the influence of puritan Brahmins who gave up vedic sacrifices and meat-eating and who took to new forms of prayer and vows (vrata-s). From Alberuni we learn that Kṣattriyas and Vaiśyas could not follow the rigorous practices of the Brāhmaṇas and only a very few of them read the Vedas. Marriage and other ceremonies were performed by them with the paurāṇik (and not the vedic) prayers; and they could not follow the advice of the Brahmins regarding prohibition of meat-eating. Hence the gulf of cultural difference between the Brahmin and other castes became too wide to admit of any intercaste marriage, though permited by the Smṛtis. The *Bṛhad-dharma-purāṇa* (edited in Bibliotheca Indica Series, which is "perhaps not much later than the 12th cent. A.D."),[236] authorises the Brahmins to eat fish and meat and divides the non-Brahmins into 36 sub-sects, each noted as a śūdra. It reflects the peculiar features of Bengal, as distinguished from the rest of North India. It describes how king Veṇa, violating the rules of varṇāśrama. created a number of mixed castes by forcing the union of males and females belonging to different castes. It shows the formation of mixed castes as in Smṛtis, formed by promiscuous union by order of the king, known as uttama, madhyama and adhama sañkaras, all having the status of śūdras. R.C. Majumdar[237] draws our attention to three categories of sub-castes and their vocations as settled by the Brahmins during the reign of Veṇa's successor and to the underlying principle viz. (1) "Those whose father and mother both belong to the four primitive castes", (2) "those whose mothers alone belong to one of the primitive castes" and (3) "those whose father and mother both belong to any mixed caste", working behind the formation of numerous sub-castes, existing as the peculiar conditions of the society in Bengal even to-day. The list of mixed castes is also available in the *Brahma-vaivarta purāṇa*. The *Brahma-vaivarta-purāṇa* mentions first śūdras and then karaṇa and ambaṣṭha and also nine castes as born of a śūdra woman by Viśvakarman, born as a Brahmin architect. It also gives us the list of degraded mixed castes like Aṭṭālikākāra (mason), Koṭaka (builder of houses), Tīvara, Tailakāra, Leṭa, Malla, Carmakāra, Śuṇḍī, Pauṇḍraka (Pod ?), Māṁsaccheda (butcher), Rājaputra, Kaivarta, Kauyālī, Gaṅgāputra, Yuṅgī (jugī) and Agari (Ugra-Kṣattriya). But even the long list of this Purāṇa is not exhaustive, because it remarks: "The mixed castes are innumerable, who can mention their names or number?" A comparative study of the castesystem, as reflected in these two Purāṇas and as prevailing in the modern society shows that the caste-system reached its final stage of evolution even in the 12th or 13th cent. A.D. Jīmūtavāhana (12th cent. A.D.) of Bengal also proves the prevalence of intercaste marriage in the society. Jīmūtavāhana says in his Dāyabhāga (tr. Colebrooke, 1898, pp. 159-161) that a male of a higher varṇa was allowed to marry a girl of a lower varṇa, even of a śūdra caste. It is shocking to learn his remark that the evils "do not ensue on the procreation of offspring upon a śūdra woman, not married to (the Brāhmaṇa) himself; but a venial offence is committed and a slight penance is requisite". That means that "though marriage with a śūdra woman involves degradation and loss of caste, illicit union with her is reckoned as a trivial offence". Śrīkṛṣṇa's commentary on this shows that "adultery with a married śūdra woman is much less heinous than marriage with her". From the above it is clear that though undesireable, the marriage of a Brahmin with a śūdra girl was prevalent in the then society and accepted as valid. Bhavadeva does not include such a marriage in the list of forbidden marriages, rather he refers to "the accomplished śūdra wife of a Brāhmaṇa" in his prāyaścitta-prakaraṇa.[238] Jīmūtavāhana also lays down rules of inheritance in case of a śūdra wife of a Brāhmaṇa and her son. Regarding the competence of wife to assist in the performance of a ritual, he mentions that a savarṇa wife alone is entitled to do so, but the wife of the caste immediately following may be employed in such duties. That means, a Vaiśya or a Śūdra wife though married to a Brāhmaṇa is not allowed to do any such religious duty. Thus a Śudra wife in such cases, though married, was not given the rank of a wife, and so this practice was gradually coming into disfavour in the society at least in the society of Bengal. Dr. Majumdar's remark in this connection deserves our attention, as quoted here: "As regards interdining and intermarriage the restrictions originally concerned only the relations between a Brāhmaṇa and low castes. It is probable that these gradually came to be regarded as marks of aristocracy or orthodoxy and were extended not only among other castes, but also among the various branches of the same caste. In the final stage, marriage was absolutely confined within the narrow fold of one of the numerous subcastes, branches or clans into which a caste was subdivided".[239]

The mythical accounts of the origin of the Kāyasthas, as found in the Rewa inscription[240] of a minister of the Kalachuri king Karṇa, dated 1049 A.D. which refers to their Śūdra origin in verses 36-38 and in the Ajaygarh record of Nāna, a minister of the Caṇḍella king Bhojavarman which traces their origin to the sage Kaśyapa, also represent the popular belief testifying to the possibility of the prevalence of the intercaste marriage in the society. We know further from the *Uśanas smṛti*[241] (ed. Anandasram Sanskrit Series) that a caste called Bhiṣak (physician) was born of illicit union of a Brāhmaṇa male with a Kṣattriya female. Ambaṣṭha is well-known to us as a mixed caste, born of a Brāhmaṇa father and a Vaiśya mother, as noted in early smṛtis. The mythical accounts of the origin of Vaidyas or Ambaṣṭhas, as noted in the *Brahmavaivarta Purāṇa* and the *Bṛhaddharma Purāṇa* also attempt to convince us of their mixed character as a result of intercaste marriage.

It is interesting to note here that kings of four main castes were entitled to offer themselves as candidates for the hands of princesses in the svayaṁbara-sabhā in ancient India and so the intercaste marriage was in practice in such cases. We may cite some examples of such matrimonial relation between kings, far and near, in ancient India, the son of Śivadeva, king of Nepal married Rājyamatī or Rājyadevī, daughter of Harṣa, king of Kāmarūpa; Dharmapāla, the Pāla emperor wedded Raññādevī, daughter of Paravala, the Rāṣṭrakūṭa king; Jātavarman, king of the Burmas took the hand of Vīraśrī the second daughter of Ċedirāj Karṇa, the marriage between Vallālasena and Ramādevī of the Cālukya dynasty and also the marriage of Mansinha, king of Ambara with Prabhāvatīdevī, sister of Lakṣmīnārāyaṇa, king of Coochbehar. Such instances remind us also of the marriage of Rajput princesses with the Moghal-Badsaha-s. The only exception is the Mewar dynasty which declined to come into such matrimonial relation with the Moghal rulers. However, such intercaste marriage did not bring about any loss of position or prestige in the society of the Kṣattriya royal families. Even today some Kṣattriya families of the kings of Kathiawar, Kutch and

Sindh are found to accept the hands of muslim princesses and the progeny of muslim princesses and the progeny of such unions are recognised as Hindus or Kṣattriyas.

REFERENCES

1. *Vision of India* (2nd ed. 1907), pp. 262-263.
2. *Character, Manners and Customs of the People of India* (London, 1817), p. 14.
3. *Hindu tribes and castes*, Vol. III, p. 293.
4. *Rv.*, x. 90.
5. *H. Ind. Lit.*, I, p. 66.
6. *Studies in Ind. Antiquities*, by H.C. Roy Choudhuri, 2nd ed., pp. 167 f.
7. 1.179.6.
8. V. 17.8 & 9.
9. *ŚB*, IV, 1, 5, 1.
10. *PB*, XIV, 6, 6.
11. 1.18.1.
12. 50-76.
13. XIII, 2, 9, 8.
14. VII, 35, 3.
15. VIII, 38, 3.
16. II, 8.1.
17. *Rv.*, 1, 126.
18. V, 17, 8 & 9.
19. III, 9, 7, 3.
20. XIII, 2, 9, 8.
21. XXX, 5.
22. IV. 2.18 .
23. *Lātyā. Ś.S.*
24. Cf. Pandit Shyam Sastri, *Evolution of Castes*, p. 4.
25. IV. 13.
26. Ch. XVI.
27. *H.D.S.*, II, pt.1 pp. 48-49.

28. *I.A.* (1911), pp. 144f.
29. XIII, 143, 50.
30. *Mbh.*, XIII, 144, 26.
31. XI, 658.
32. *navai brāhmaṇo rājyāyālam*, *ŚB*, V. 1,1,2. *na vai brāhmaṇe strī ramate"* - *TS*, III, 9, 14.
33. *Studies in Kauṭilya*, pp. 161-162.
34. *Caste in India* tr. by Ross, p. 124.
35. *H.D.S.*, II (pt.1), p. 447.
36. *AB*, VIII, 1.
37. 4, 1, 5, 9.
38. V. 50.
39. *ŚB* - XIII, 2, 9, 8; Cf. Vs, 26, 30.
40. XII, 13; Cf. *Kāṭh. Saṃ*. 21.7.
41. 18, 17-18.
42. 1. 56.
43. V. 4, 9
44. II, 1, 15; Cf. *Kauṣītaki Brā.*, i up, IV. 18.
45. IV. 4, 28.
46. II, 6, 13, 1, 3-4.
47. 1.4.
48. IV. 20.
49. 1, 8.2-5 of *Mbh.*, Anu, 44, 11-13.
50. I. 63.
51. *Vana*, 122.
52. *Ibid.*, 115, 21 and Anu, 4, 19.
53. *Ibid.*, 113
54. *Ibid.*, 97
55. *Ibid.*, 116, 2.
56. 1, 81, 31.
57. *Ibid.*
58. *Mbh.* 1, 114, 12-13.
59. *Mbh.* I, 71 & 72.
60. *Mbh.* Adi, 187, 23.
61. *Mbh.* Adi, 100 chap.

62. *Mbh.* Droṇa, 69, 3.
63. *Mbh.* Sānti, 171, 5.
64. *Mbh.*, Ādi, 29, 3.
65. *Mbh.*, Anu, 44, 12.
66. *Mbh.*, Anu, 48, 4.
67. *Mbh.*, Ādi, 128, 65.
68. *Mbh.*, Ādi, 120, 33-35.
69. *Mbh.*, Anu, ch. 49.
70. *Mbh.*, Ādi, 106, 32. and 114, 14. Cf. *Mbh.*, (Ādi), ed. *H.D.S.*, 114, 35.
71. *Mbh.*, Ādi, 106, 32; and 114, 14.
72. *Mbh.*, Ādi, 41, 5.
73. *Mbh.*, Śānti, Ch. 296 and Anu, Ch. 48.
74. IV, 16-21
75. 1, 8, 6; 1, 9, 3.
76. II, 1, 2, 6; II, 4, 9, 5,
77. Ch. 28.
78. X. 6.
79. X, 155.
80. 1,16,6.
81. X, 12 & 16.
82. X, 25.
83. X, 24.
84. X, 32 f.
85. X, 35.
86. Manu, X, 38
87. *J.*, I, 199
88. *J.*, III, 93.
89. 1, 5, 1.*Forms of Marriage*
90. *J.*, V. 211.
91. *J.*, III. 81.
92. *J.*, II, 5.
93. *KS*, 5-26.
94. *AŚ*, ed. Shamasastry (1929), p. 187.
95. *AŚ*, VI, Book-III, p. 184 f.

96. 1, 90.
97. *Yāj.*, 1, 91-92.
98. *Yāj.*, 1, 95.
99. *H.D.S.*, II, pt. 1, p. 54, fn. 127.
100. *H.D.S.*, II, pt. 1, pp. 55-56.
101. 16.2.
102. 1, 91.
103. *Soc. Life in Anc. India*, p. 16.
104. II, 62, 14-15.
105. ed. Majumdar, p. 311.
106. *JA* (1926), pp. 1-55.
107. *P.H.A.I.*, p. 207.
108. *J.*, IV, 363.
109. X. 47.
110. Cf. Risley's *People of India*, p. 114.
111. 37.7.
112. III. 8.
113. Vol. II, ch. 1, 120-21.
114. *SBE*, XXV, p. 403, fn. 7, Cf *Mitā.* on Yāj., 1, 91.
115. 1.9.5.
116. 1.1.4, 8.
117. *Mīmāṁsāsūtra*, VI, 1, 44-50.
118. 1.9.6.
119. 1.95.
120. X, 47.
121. VIII, 42, 48.
122. II, 21.
123. V, 5.
124. *SBE*, vol. 33, p. 375.
125. VIII, 6-7.
126. *Society and Admini. of India* (Cal. 1967), p. 108.
127. p. 19. *Domanaḥ pāla-jāmātā Vaidyaḥ Pālo na Vidyate.*
128. Candraprabhā, p. 4.
129. *Soc. and Admin. of India*, p. 126.
130. *Anc. Ind. Soc. Hist.* (N. Delhi, 1978), p. 127 f.

131. *E.I.*, IX, p. 6 f.
132. *I.A.*, 39, p.191 f.
133. 18.3.
134. X. 39.
135. X. 15.
136. Mauṣalaparvan, 7, 46-63 and 8, 16-17.
137. Āśvamedhira, 29, 15-16.
138. On Pāṇ. 1, 2, 72.
139. *Kāvyādarśa*, 1.3.6.
140. Cf. Diksalkar D.B., *Proc. 5th Ori. Conf.*, 1930, vol. 1, p. 565.
141. Lüd.'s List No. 1137.
142. 1.8.8.
143. 1, 9, 15.
144. 1, 8, 12.
145. X, 18.
146. *A.Ś.* III, 7.
147. *A.Ś.*, III, 7.
148. V, 10, 7.
149. *Gaut.*, IV. 15-16; *Manu*, X, 12; *Yāj.*, 1, 93, Anuśāsana, 48, 11.
150. 29, 17.
151. 1, 1, 3,12.
152. 1, 9, 6.
153. X, 32.
154. Virāṭ, 9, 18-19. and Vana, 65, 68-70.
155. *Hist. Anc. Bengal*, p. 416.
156. *Camb. Hist. of India*, 1, ch. XVII.
157. IV, 724.
158. X, 43-44.
159. *The Guhilas of Kiskindhā*, p. 17.
160. *Early Brāhmī Records in India*, H.P. Chakraborti, p. 10.
161. *Ibid.* p. 17.
162. Lüd. List No. 994.
163. *Succ. Sat*, L. Decc, (Sircar), pp. 22-23.
164. *Lüd.* No. 29.
165. Lüd. Nos. 1099 & 1131.

166. *S.I.*, p. 179.
167. *S.I.*, p. 178.
168. *E.I.*, vol. 34, p. 20 f.
169. Bhandarkar's list of inscriptions, no.1736.
170. *E.I.*, Vol. 34, p. 245.
171. *Succ. Sat.*, p. 135.
172. Bhandarkar's List. No. 1708 and *S.I.*, p. 478.
173. ed. T. Watter, London, 1908, II, 246.
174. Ray, *DHNI*, 1, pp. 288, 304 etc.
175. *Ibid.*, p. 518.
176. *E.I.*, XVIII, p. 17.
177. *A.S.W.I.*, IV, p. 140.
178. *E.I.*, XV, pp. 301 f.
179. *E.I.*, XV, p. 12 and XVIII, p. 17.
180. XII, 4852 f.
181. Foreign Elements in the Hindu population, *IA*, XL (1911), pp.3-37.
182. XIII, 4, 48.
183. *Viṣṇu-purāṇa*, IV, 19, 10.
184. Ch. 296; Cf. Anuśāsana, ch. 48.
185. *Caste and Class of India*, pp. 59 and 80.
186. *Rāmāyaṇa*, Ayodhyā, 63, 51.
187. *Ibid.*, 64, 24.
188. *S.B. Buddhists*, vol. II.
189. Ucchvāsa, I.
190. Watters, I, p. 168.
191. p. 148.
192. *The Classical Age* (U. Ghoshal), p. 561 and fn.
193. pp. 83 f. and 148.
194. p. 187.
195. *DKC*, p. 68, *ASK*, p. 200.
196. *DKC*, pp. 69-72.
197. *DKC*, p. 160.
198. IV, 18-19.
199. Cf. *H.D.S.*, II, pt. 1, pp. 62-63.

200. II, 11, 10-11.
201. 1, 8, 13-14
202. X, 64
203. *H.D.S.*, II, pt. 1, pp. 63-64
204. I, 96.
205. I, 118.
206. X, 1-7.
207. II, 22-23.
208. 32, 1724.
209. Anu, 48, 4.
210. III,43-44.
211. 8.6.
212. 26, 1-3.
213. IX, 23-24.
214. Vyāsa, 1, 7, 8.
215. 18, 1-5.
216. IX, 153.
217. IX, 155.
218. On *Yāj.*, II,125
219. III, 6.
220. 28, 43.
221. 15, 37.
222. *Sachau*, II, p. 156.
223. IV, 15-42.
224. *Rāja.*, V, 206.
225. *Rāja.*, V. 387.
226. *Kathā.*, 53, 108.
227. *Ibid.*, 25, 171.
228. *Rāja.*, 1,318.
229. *C.M.I.*, pt. IV, No. 11.
230. *Rāja.*, VIII, 10.
231. 19, 3.
232. Ch. 22.
233. Ch.6.
234. 15, 16-18.

235. *Uśanas*, 6, 35.
236. *H.B.* (ed. R.C. Maunder), p. 410.
237. *Ibid.*, pp. 417-419.
238. Ed. Girish Chandra Vidyāratna, pub. 241. Verse 26. Varendra Research Society, Rajshahi, p. 90.
239. *H.B.*, p. 426.
240. *E.I.*, XXIV, 101 f.
241. Verse 26.

CHAPTER - V

Impact of Islam

We have noted before that other foreign invaders in the early centuries of the Christian era settled here and were gradually absorbed into the Hindu society. But the Muslims were eager to convert Indians to their faith instead of being so absorbed in the Hindu society. From the 7th cent. A.D. onwards, the Muslim traders from Persia and Arab came and settled in western coast of India and they married the women of this country specially in Malabar and Saurāṣṭra. The Muslim saints followed these traders and by their pious and austere lives exercised a great influence over the Hindus. During the Muslim rule the process of conversion went on and many lowclass Hindus were easily won over to be converted into Islam. But in spite of some defects, the castesystem of the Hindus which became still more rigid, saved Hinduism from being assimilated into Islam. The Muslim rule brought a further deterioration of the position of women. The breakdown of social institutions, inevitable result of continuous invasion, upsetting of traditional political structures and economic depression led to the general depression of social life: specially among women.

With the advent of the Muslims in India the Brahmins who were the recognised custodians of Hindu culture, tried to protect, not by liberalising its doctrines and improving it spiritually but by laying stress on purity of birth and non-connection with foreign blood. Hence we learn of some 'Kalivarjya-s in our scriptures of which the important factor was disallowing intercaste marriage'. The different Rajput clans, about thirty-six like the Chauhans, the Vaghelas, the Devaḍas, the Solankis and others, as described in Kānhaḍade-prabandha regarded themselves as Kṣattriyas by the beginning of the medieval period, though some of them had not forgotten their non-kṣattriya origin in the earlier age. These clans intermarried, whether settled in Gujarat or Madhya Pradesh. We learn of different theories about the origin of the Chauhans. Tod[1] regarded them as descendants of the non-Aryan Takṣakas. The Agnikula myth is explained by W. Crooke as representing "a rite of purgation by fire" by which "The impurity of the foreigners was removed and they became fitted to enter the Hindu caste system".[2] But the inscriptions of the so-called Agnikula races record that the Pratihāra-s of Mandsor were the descendants of a Brahmin Hariścandra and his Kṣattriya wife, Bhadrā[3] and that the Pāramāras of the Vasiṣṭha branch of the Abu races. Bhandarkar[4] thinks that the Chauhāns were Khazars and originally belonged to a priestly section of some foreign tribes. But Rājaśekhara's marriage with Avantīsundarī, a Chauhān Lady is an instance of anuloma marriage between a Brahmin and a Kṣattriya. Saṁgrāmarāja[5] of Kashmir gave his daughter in marriage to a Brahmin. The Guhila-s were also originally Brahmins and they were noted as Brāhmaṇas upto the time of Mahārāṇā Kumbha.[6] The Hūnas, noted in *Kumārapāla-caritam* and *Kanhaḍa prabandha* as ruling families were actually foreign immigrants into India from Central Asia. Thus many Brāhmaṇas became founders of Rajput families. Uśanas[7] says that a Brāhmaṇa's sons by a kṣattriya wife is regarded as a Kṣattriya. (*nṛpāyāṃ vidhinā viprāj-jāto nṛpa iti smṛtaḥ*). The assimilation of foreign fighting tribes into the kṣattriya fold of the Hindu society was made possible no less by intermarriage, as evidenced by the earlier instances of Rudradāman getting his daughter married to a Sātavāhana prince of South India, and of Samudragupta taking wives from the Kuṣāṇas and Sākas (royal families). Yasaḥkarṇa Chedi was the son of a Hūna princess.[8] The Guhila ruler, Allaṭa of Mewar had a queen belonging to the family of "Hūnakṣonīśa" (Hūna-ruler).[9] D. Sharma[10] remarks that "the Katris were probably a pratiloma class, born of a Kṣattriya father and a brahmin mother", as evidenced by the tradition current in Rajasthan. Some of the Gurjaras of Rajasthan were regarded as Kṣattriyas. The Baḍ-Gurjaras, obviously Gurjaras were counted as one of 36 Rajput clans who used to intermarry with them. The Jaina Bhaṇḍāris of Marwar regard themselves as descendants of Lakṣaṇa of Nāḍol and one of his Vaiśya queens.[11] Khargadhara of Bhoja of Ranthambhor is said to have been related to Hammira in the same way as Vidura to Pāṇḍu.

REFERENCES

1. *Annals and Antiquity of Rajasthan*, 1. p. 80.
2. *Early Hist. of India*, (3rd ed.), p. 412.
3. *I.I.*, XVIII, p. 95.
4. *J.A.*, XLI, pp. 25-29.
5. *Rājataraṅgini*, VII, 10-12.
6. D.R. Bhandarkar, *JRASB*, 1909; *I.H.R.* XXVIII, 83 f.
7. V. 28.
8. *E.I.*, XII, p. 212.
9. *I.A.*, XXXIX, p. 191.
10. *Purātana-prabandha-saṅgraha*, p. 102.
11. *Hamira-mahākāvya*, IX, verses 153-155.

CHAPTER - VI

Interracial Mixture

Now let us enquire into interracial mixture which took place in India from the earliest times. Though ethnology and anthropology have grown up as a modern science, our forefathers have left some traces of knowledge of these subjects in their own writings, as they could distinguish people of different stock. The first attempt at such distinction was made by R.P. Chanda in his "Indo Aryan Races", published in 1916 wherein he studied culture of Āryas and anāryas of the Vedic India and particularly that of the Aryans of the inner and outer band.

R. Shafer's "Ethnography of Ancient India" (1954) is a new contribution in the field of ethnological study, of course on the basis of language. Such study of man on the basis of physiological factors, language and sociological characteristics is a difficult task, no doubt. H. Risley[1] divides the people of India into seven classes: Turko-Iranian, Indo-Aryan, Scytho-Dravidian, Arya-Dravidian, Mongola-Dravidian, Mongoloid Dravidian. W. Hunter[2] speaks of two branches of the Dravidians (i) the Kolarian-speaking dialects allied to Muṇḍa and (ii) the Dravidians proper who used dialect allied to Tamil. B.S. Guha speaks of "six main races with nine sub-types in his "Racial Elements in the population", published in 1944:

1. The Negrito
2. The Proto-Austroloid
3. The Mongoloid (i) Paleo-and (ii) Tibeto-Mongoloids.
4. The Mediterranean (i) Paleo-, (ii) Mediterranean and (iii) the so-called Oriental type.

5. The Western Brachycephals (i) Alpinoid, (ii) Dinaric and (iii) Armenoid.
6. The Nordic.

S.K. Chatterjee[3] again divides the above six classes of people to four types on the basis of language: (i) Austric, spoken by the aboriginal tribes, (ii) Dravidian used by the people of South India, (iii) Sino-Tibetan, spoken by people of north and north-east of India and (iv) Aryan or Indo-European, used by people of north India, north-western frontier; belonging to the Mediteranean of the Punjab, and Upper Gānges Valley-taller and fairer, and to the Oriental type, found in the Punjab, Rajasthan, Sind and U.P. and also to the Nordics of these regions. If Chatterjee is right, the Aryans must have been a mixture of at least three ethnic elements, noted above. But R. Shafer[4] warns us that "it is very difficult to distinguish carefully between race and language". B.S. Guha[5] also observes: "There is no justification for giving a racial meaning to such terms as 'Dravidian' and 'Austric' as J. Przyluski and some of his followers have done".

The ārya-varṇa and dāsa or dasyu-varṇa, noted in the Ṛgveda and discussed before indicate the ethnic differences between white people, the Nordics and the aboriginal black people with whom the Nordic Aryans had to fight in the earliest phase of Vedic culture and who are referred to as Proto-Australoids by R.P. Chanda.[6] The epithet anāsa, applied to Dāsa-Dasyus' shows that these people were Proto-Mongoloids as well.

From the description of the battle of ten kings in the Ṛgveda we learn that Sudās, the Bharata king had to fight two battles, one on the Paruṣṇī (the Ravi) and another on the Yamunā and in both fields he won victory. His enemies on the west were Puru, Yadu, Turvaśa, Anu, Druhyu, Alina, Paktha, Bhalānas, Śiva and Viṣānin; while his eastern enemies were Aja, Sigru and Yakṣu, evidently totemistic Proto-Australoid tribes. From the ethnological standpoint we may interpret the above incident as showing that the people lying to the west of the Ravi were Proto-Iranian broad heads using Iranian or Dardic language and the Harappans consisting of the Mediterraneans, Proto-Australoids,

Proto-Nordics, and Mongoloids, the people of the region, east of the Yamunā were either the Proto-Australoids or of the Sino-Tibetan stock, that the Nordics lived in the area from the Ravi to the Yamunā and also that the broad-headed Dardics occupied the region lying north of the Bharata territory. Some scholar thinks that "the eastern Ganges basin was occupied by the Tibeto-Burmans, "while" the Ganges-Yamuna valley was under the Proto-Australoids, who, however, seem to have extended further east, as the names Aṅga-Vaṅga etc. show, till they were dislodged from the region by the Mongoloids". R.P. Chanda[9] opines that tribes like Yadu, Turvaśa, Anu, Druhyu and Puru belong to the Alpine group and in India they were mixed with the Nordics. If so, there happened interracial mixture in this region in the Ṛgvedic age. The various finds "in Mohenjodaro and Harappa indicate a number of racial types. They may be provisionally identified as the proto-Australoid, Mediterranean, Proto-Nordics, and Mongoloids:".[10] R.P. Chanda says that the Yadus, Turvaśas and others belonged to the Alpine stock. The skeletal remains show that the Aryans and non-Aryans (dāsa-s) lived when both of them had to fight with the Bharatas of the Sarasvatī valley.

The Takman verse of the *Atharva-veda* (22.5.14) shows an attitude of hostility from the Indo-Nordics (Aryans) of the interior of the sub-continent towards the people of border areas like Gandhāra, Mujavants, Bālhikas in the west and also the eastern peoples like Magadha and Aṅga. There is no doubt that the Indo-Nordics were intermarried with these non-Aryan people as a result of which new tribes like the Kurus came into being as evidenced by the *Śatapatha Brāhmaṇa*. Śibi Auśinara, referred to in the Ṛgveda[12] also show how the Uśinaras and the Śibis (Greek Siboi) were mixed together. Grierson[13] points out that the Kafirs and Dards came earlier than the Nordics and were mixed with the latter, before the Nordics marched eastward and settled in Videha region. In the later Vedic period the fusion between the pre-Aryans and the Aryans, not only racial but also cultural led to the rise of priests and their superiority to the warriors. Some scholar thinks that the term asura refers to the Ahuras or Iranians and if so, the āsura form of marriage was prevalent among the Indians under the influence of Iranian ideal. But the *Gītā* (XVI. 6) speaks of two types of men with Daivī and āsurī qualities. The second denotes what is unrighteous. Hence the Dharma texts denounce this form of marriage, though prevailing in the Indian society. From the epics we learn that Gāndhārī and Kaikeyī were taken from their guardians in exchange of huge amount of money and so we may presume that some of the north-western tribes followed this practice after the Iranian fashion. The Rākṣasa and Paiśāca are both ethnic terms and these are generally applied to some tribes of the proto-Australoid group in the style of condemnation. It is difficult to determine how far this Paiśāca form is associated with the speakers of the Paiśācī prākṛta, now represented by the Dards and other tribes of the N.W. frontier of Pakistan. However, it may not be unlikely that these forms of marriage crept into Aryan society under the influence of some pre-Aryan tribes. Foreign hordes poured into Indian soil from outside even in the historical period and were gradually Indianised and incorporated into the framework of Varṇa-system of the Aryan society, as evidenced by the theory of aṇuloma and pratiloma, enunciated in the Dharma literature. Manu (X. 20-23) speaks of different types of Vrātyas varṇa-wise showing the degradation as a result of deviation from the Aryan ideal. Thus we are sure of the fact that admixture of blood had been going on in Indian society from very early times and particularly from the days of infiltration of foreigners into the Indian society in the historical period.[14]

To cite some instances, the term Yavana may be considered. Gautama mentions it as an offspring of a Kṣattriya father and a Śūdra mother but Manu means by this a Kṣattriya, degraded to the status of a Śūdra. Evidently the Greeks came to India along with Alexander and some settled here and were Indianised. They became also the ruling class and so were accepted as Kṣattriya-s but degraded to the lowest order. Similarly the Ābhīra-s,[15] a Central Asiatic tribe came to India during or as a result of confusion created by Alexander's death. They are noted in the

Mahābhārata[16] as untouchable Śūdras but as one of a little higher status, not untouchable in *Mahābhāṣya*.[17] Manu speaks of them as born of a Brāhmaṇa on the daughter of an Ambaṣṭha. Kṛṣṇa is said to have been dallying with Ābhīra girls in the *Bhāgavata-purāṇa*. Hence we may safely conclude that foreigners like the Greeks and Central Asian tribes were Indianised gradually after they had settled here after 323 B.C. and they were obviously intermarried with the indigenous people. Indrāgnidatta of western Indian cave inscriptions calls himself a Greek but not only he but also his father bears an Indian name, showing thereby the admixture of blood.

The Scythians came to India from the Russian Turkestan area after the Greek rule in India. Risley[19] says that they came "from a region occupied exclusively by broad-headed races". S. Levi[20] speaks of the Śaka Muruṇḍas in Eastern India on the basis of the Chinese and Jaina evidences and of Ptolemy's Geography. Evidently the presence of broad-head in the Saṁkīrṇa-yoni region was due to the infiltration of the Scythians into the Indian society. The *Mahābhārata*[21] speaks of the foreign tribes, mostly of Central Asia that came and settled in India as "several castes that have originated from the Brāhmaṇas, the Kṣattriyas, the Vaiśyas and śūdras that live in the dominions of Aryan kings", and that "they live like dasyus". Elsewhere the same source[22] speaks of them as fallen kṣattriyas, degraded into śūdras, obviously reflecting their life and position in Indian society of two different periods. From all these evidences it is clear that both the Jāti and Varṇa theories had been operating in the then Indian society when foreign tribes were by slow degrees assimilated into it, not only by intermixture of blood but also of culture.

We may discuss, by the bye, how among a few people in the eastern division of India some sort of hybrid culture grew up from very early times. *Bodhāyana D.S.* and Manu[23] speaks that a Māgadha is an offspring of a Kṣattriya mother and a Vaiśya father; evidently indicating the fusion of Aryan blood. F.E. Pargiter[24] says that in Magadha the Aryans mixed up with some invaders who came over the sea from the east. Hence, we may think of the people of Magadha as Proto-Australoid at the base, but mixed up with the Aryan blood later on. We know from the *ŚB* how the Aryan culture penetrated into Videha through Videgha Māthava who carried Agni from the Kośala country crossing the Sadānīrā river to Videha. From the *Ṛgveda* we learn that Kośala was already under the Yadus and Turvaśas and so the colonists, headed by Māthava was already a mixed race. From the remark of S.K. Chatterjee[25] on the Licchavis we may presume that the Licchavis were Indo-Mongoloids, having Tibeto-Burman or Sino-Tibetan elements and that all the non-Aryan speakers of this region were mixed up with the Aryan-speaking people after the infiltration of Aryan culture there. Small republican tribes lying north of the Ganges and on the border of the Himalayas, as referred to in the Pāli texts indicate that they belonged to the same stocks as the Licchavis.

Similarly Surāṣṭra in Western India is noted in the *Mahābhārata*[26] as the country of the people of mixed origin (saṁkara). From the Purāṇas we learn that the Yadava Sātvata had shifted from Mathura to this region. Naturally they belonged to the race of broad heads. The Periplus refers to Abhiria and its sea-board Syrastrene (sec. 41) and thus mentions the Ābhīras of Surāṣṭra. The Ābhīras are spoken of as Śūdras in the *Mahābhāratā*. The Periplus also mentions the natives of Ariaca district as "men of larger stature and coloured black". Thus these evidences of the *Mbh.* and the Periplus, taken together lead us to conclude that the broad heads of this region had mixed up with the foreign Ābhīras and other early black people of the locality.

The Avantī region is closely associated with the Yādavas (of broad heads) in the Purāṇas.[27] The Yādavas uprooted the Nāgas who had already annihilated the Proto-Australoids there. The Burusaski Language is still spoken in Hunza region. Long ago Grierson, on the basis of that had opined that the Nāgas were the speakers of that language and they were ancestors of the non-Aryan inhabitants of Hunza Nagar.

Many foreign tribes like Cīna, Kirāta,Tuṣāra and others as low and barbarous became Indianised and mixed up with the native people of India and they are classified ethnologically in the Purāṇas. Risley has divided the people of Uttarāpatha into two groups: (i) the Turko-Iranian type in N.W.F., Balucistan and the region lying west of the Indus and (ii) the Indo-Aryan type in Kashmir, the Punjab and Rajputna. This Uttarāpatha region, though dominated by foreign tribes had many colonies of Kṣattriyas (*kṣattriyopaniveśāśca*) and of Śūdra (*śūdrakulāni ca*), corresponding to the Xathroi and the Sodroi of the classical authors.

To sum up the above discussions, we may conclude on the basis of anthropological study that no one in India can claim to have a pure racial origin, that is, he is after all a mixed product. Linguistic study also helps us to know that the Indians speaking various tongues may be broadly subdivided into four main groups: Austric, Dravidian, Tibeto-Mongoloid and Aryan. That means, India was prey to racial admixtures from very early times, as early as the Ṛgvedic period. India is indeed more a continent than a country, enriched with diverse elements in language, religion and culture but having one underlying unity in the midst of diversities. India is known as Bhāratavarṣa (one territorial division) where all are conceived of as descendants of king Bharata, as noted in the *Vāyu-purāṇa* (45, 75). The Vedic Aryans came in contact with the pre-Aryans belonging to the Proto-Australoid, Mediterranean, and other stocks who were numerically stronger. However, the people of different stocks mixed together and evolved a new society by following the policy of give and take, on the basis of the caste-system which as noted before, operated in two ways of varṇa and jāti, varṇa meaning colour or character indicating occupational castes and jāti determining one's caste by birth. Then even an alien element was culturally conquered and admitted into the social field by the ways of his work or occupation. The Dharma texts mention the main four castes and then numerous subcastes, sometimes after the names of different tribes and occupational groups, interpreted as offsprings of intercaste marriage amongst them. The foreign tribes were thus Aryanised and incorporated into the framework of Aryan castesystem, but they were allowed to maintain some social practices and customs of their own. Thus the orthodox caste system absorbed diverse racial elements within its own fold. F.G. Bailey's remark deserves mention: "We can define caste and tribe in such a way that they are one, but this oneness will be verbal, not real. Underlying both tribes and caste societies are identical principles. But these principles are differently applied and if we ignore this fact we have lost touch with reality".[28] The policy of the Hindus, according to N.K. Bose[29] was not to eradicate the old beliefs and practices where they were not inconsistent with Brahmanical moral ideas..... The Brahmins modifed the old culture where it went against the grain of their own ideas and left the rest intact". S. Chattopadhyaya rightly points out in his "Traditional values in Indian life, 12 that unity in diversity in the cultural life of India was brought about by the system of varṇa through the medium of which foreigners and non-aryan groups of India found their way into the social order without creating any disturbance in the general life of the people".

Endogamy, i.e. the principle of marrying inside the group is compulsory for the orthodox section of the Aryans who do not allow any admixture of blood of the diverse groups. But we have discussed how far the Aryans relaxed their strict code of mariage and allowed intercaste or even interracial marriage, only to accommodate the different ethnic groups within the Hindu fold. At present Hindu marriage may be recognised as either of two forms, Brāhma, i.e. gift of the girl or Āsura, i.e. some sort of sale of the girl. Even the aboriginal tribes follow some of the principles of the higher section of the people like bride price and the Hindu custom of child marriage, as prevailing among the Bhils of Gujarat, Gwalior and the adjoining areas.[30] Similar practices may be found out among the people of the lower section of the Rāḍh area.

It is interesting to note that child marriage and the guardians' predominant role in the arrangement of marriage, of course, were the traditional fashion of the orthodox society; of course, child marriage has been restrained by legislation, as discussed before but guardian-s' role is still persisting in the society, both high and low. But in cases of intercaste marriage the decision of the parties, both the groom and the bride is gaining greater importance, sometimes with and sometimes even against the will or consent of the legal guardians. From the census reports we learn of not less than three thousand castes or subcastes in India, each forming an endogamous group. Sometimes geographical isolation led to the formation of separate groups like Rāḍhi and Vārendra among the same class of the Brāhmaṇas and the two were not allowed to be married until recently. In South India the Nambudri Brahmins are subdivided owing to hostility between cultures with matrilineal and patrilineal modes of descent.

There is no denying the fact that caste system produces some evil effects on the social life of the Indians. It subdivides the social organisms into smaller and smaller sections, each looking to the interests of its own group, to the utter neglect of those of the entire community and each considering itself superior to all others. But scholars like Hutton draw our notice to the brighter aspect of the caste-system: "it has proved capable of absorbing any intrusive society .." Manu (ch. x) shows how caste system unified diverse ethnic groups of India into one social body so much so that it has counteracted the influence of proselytising Islam in the later periods of Indian history and has saved India from the conversion of the 3/4th of the population into Islam and from the clutches of the Christian missionaries. Of course, Indian society is both static and dynamic, because while the caste system has made the people of India more conservative, it has assimilated many foreign elements of Iranian, Greeco-Scythian, Parthian, Islamic and even of cultures of both the eastern and western world.

The Central Government of India has declared equality to all citizens and pledged to establish a casteless society. The Government has passed many laws to create conditions to achieve this goal. Intercaste marriage or even inter-racial unions would usher in an era of class-less life in India. Laws for the eradication of untouchability has been passed and the Indian Congress has all along, under the guidance and inspiration of Mahatma Gandhi and his worthy followers like Jawaharlal Nehru and Rajendra

Prasad, fought against it. Even among the untouchables there are many castes and sub-castes of various grades. As for example, the Holeyas (untouchables) of Mysore "will not take food or drink touched by the smiths, though the latter are now declaring themselves to be Viśvakarmā brahmiṇs".

Tribal endogamy is the general rule of these tribes. But marriage is allowed between tribes of an inferior order and those of a superior one and even the Hindu castes. Here also the tribes maintain territorial endogamy and the endogamous groups do not intermarry, because of the varying degree of Hinduisation. The tribes, more Hinduised pride on their superiority and refuse intermarriage with those, less Hinduised; and such gradation is found among the Gond, Bhil, Bhilala, Korku and Muṇḍa and others. The primitive tribes in Assam live in patrilineal clanṣ and practise clan-and kinship-exogamy, though some of them allow inter-clan marriage.

Matriarchal system still exists in Malabar and in Assam. Some think of the probable connection of South Indian matriarchal system with the Indus valley culture or with the same society in East Africa or Arabia. Many low castes and tribes of the hills of Malabar follow the same system of their overlords, the Nair. A girl can marry even a member of a different caste of equal or higher social rank. It is intresting to note that only the eldest brother of the Nambudiri Brahmins could marry a girl of his own caste, while others married Nair girls. Girls of Tiya and Mukkuvan married Europeans and Arabs respectively. But now under new economic conditions the Nair are forced to leave their native places and shift to a new place; and so, they fail to continue the past matriarchal system, specially in towns and outside Malabar. The people like the Khasi, Synteng and Garo in Assam live still in matriarchal society.

Another view of the system of marriage among the tribes in India is presented here. Some tribes of South India like the Kadar, the Kanikar, the Hill Pantaram, the Ulladan, Vishavan, the Urali and others settle their marriage through their parents or other relatives. But marriage by capture is common among the Mannan and Badaga and frequent among the Muduvan. Marriage by elopement is common among the Kadar, Mannan and Urali. Exchange of sisters is common among the Vishavan. Premarital sex-relations are sanctioned by almost all tribes. Some tribes like the Kadar and Nayadi practise compulsory monogamy. Polyandry is allowed among the Muduvan, Urali and Mannan.

Most of these tribes prefer cross-cousin marriage particularly among the Hill-Pantaram, Nayadi and Muduvan. Tribal endogamy is practised by almost all of them, except the Kadar who allow their women to be married with the estate labourers of the plains. Stephen Fuchs[31] remarks: "Usually the tribes of a lower social status accept marriage-partners from tribes or castes of a higher social status". Some of these tribes or castes follow the principle of territorial endogamy, that is, they can marry within the groups of a certain area. But the rules of exogamy vary, some tribes like the Hill Pantaram have two groups of three or four families, each in one locality, and these are exogamous. The Nakikar allow intermarriage among two only of four clans, one of the higher category and another of the lower one but the members of a higher clan can not intermarry ones of the lower one. The primitive tribes of Central India like the Śabaras, the Koi, the Baiga, Gond and Bhil arrange their marriage mostly though parents or guardians and practise different forms of marriage, as in South India, though marriage by purchase is still the most popular form. The Bhils of Gujarat and Rajasthan are divided into two broad groups: (i) the hagas including brothers, cousins and others on the paternal side and marriage between two hagas is not allowed and (ii) the hagwadia-consisting of the marriageable relatives and before any marriage alliance one has to be assured whether one of the two is a Haga or a Hagwadia. The Santhals,one of the three largest tribal groups of India at present live mostly in W. Bengal, Bihar and Orissa. Their concept of kinship is also very keen. Each clan is divided into two groups, one of common blood between whom there can be no marriage and the other, Bandhu Pera with whom they may be married.

REFERENCES

1. *The People of India* (Calcutta, 1908), 34 ff.
2. *The Indian Empire*, Vol. 1, 378.
3. *Vedic Age*, ed. Majumdar and Altekar, p. 145.
4. *Ethnography of Anc. India*, 5, fn. 1.
5. *Racial Elements in the Population*, p. 27.
6. *The Indo-Aryan Races*, pp. 6-7.
7. VII, 18-20.
8. R. Shafer, *Ethnography of Anc. India*, p. 13.
9. *Indo-Aryan Races*, 33.
10. D.M. Majumdar, *Races and Culture of India* (Bombay, 10 p. 26; ASIR, 1962).
11. XII, 9, 3, 3.
12. *RV*. X, 173 ascribed by Anukramaṇī.
13. *Linguistic Survey of India*, 102.
14. D.R. Bhandarkar, Foreign Elements in Hindu population, in *Ind. Ant.*, (1911).
15. Tarn, *The Greeks in Bactria and India* (1951, Camb. Uni. Press), pp. 171-172.
16. *Mbh.*, XI, 87.1
17. I. 25.
18. *Manu*, X. 15.
19. *The People of India* (Calcutta, 1908), p. 59.
20. Deux Peuples Méconnus in Melanges Charles des Harlez, 176-85.
21. Śāntiparvan, ch. 65.
22. Anuśāsanaparvan, ch. 33.
23. X, II.
24. *J.R.A.S.*, 1908, 85 ff.
25. *Kirāta-jana-Kṛti* (Calcutta, 1951), 25.
26. VIII, 30, 61 ff.
27. *A.I.N.T.*, 280.
28. *Contributions to Indian Sociology*, V, 19.
29. *Cultural Anthropology*, 166.
30. D.N. Majumdar, *Races and Cultures of India*, 193-4.
31. *The Origin of Man and Culture*, Bombay, 1963, p. 130, by Stephen Fuchs.

PART - III

CHAPTER - VII

Intercaste Marriage in Modern India

A brief survey of the Social reform movement in modern Indian history is necessary to assess the impact of the reform particularly in intercaste marriage. The movements for the reform in the society in the 19th century in India was started by the individual reformers. They raised their lone voice against many evil practices and customs which were prevalent in the society. Of course, such attempt at social reform does not mean any thorough going reorganisation of the social structure, as in the West, for the good of the toiling millions of the land but it was mainly a movement for the preservation of the society and at the same time the transformation of its members, specially with an eye to the lower classes and women folk. To state more precisely, though the reformers knew the evils of caste system in India, they did not try to eliminate it as a whole and what they insisted on, is a change in the basic value of a society and they paid more attention to different problems of marriage like widow-marriage, age-restriction in marriage, dowry-system, interdining and intermarriage etc.

Sudhiranjan Das[1] presents some aspects of the 19th cent. Bengali society: 'As each father tried to give his daughter in marriage to kulīn, the non-kulīns experienced great difficulty in procuring wives. They had to purchase wives for themselves. This led to the practice of bride-price. This form of selling girls became so common that it soon turned into a flourishing business with the Brahmanical community. The Brahmins started collecting girls from other castes and creeds and passed them on as their own daughters. It is recorded in the newspaper letters of 1837 that once two Brahmins, while travelling in Burdwan came across a charming girl whom they wanted to buy. Understanding the desire of these Brahmins a Yavana (muslim) told them that the said girl belonged to the muslim community. Even then the Brahmins agreed to purchase the girl by rupees four. She was immediately clothed with a new śāḍī, purchased from the local market. On that very night she was sold and given in marriage. Next morning she was taken to her husband's house, one day the new wife accidentally uttered some words indicating her affiliation with the muslim community. Being hard pressed, she had no other alternative but to confess that she was a muslim girl. Further we learn that a certain Mukhopadhyay Brahmin of Calcutta married a girl born of a Brahmin (upapatnī) concubine of a saheb (an Englishman). By that union she had a daughter who was later on given in marriage to a pure Rāḍhī brahmin. Similarly we learn from other records that two brahmins married girls who were later on detected to be daughter of a Mālākar. Even at Bhatpara, the home of orthodox brahmins a brahmin married a girl by purchase. It was only after a long time that he could find out that his wife was the daughter of a Pod, a low and untouchable caste. All these accounts are full of sociological import. They show how so many low-caste and muslim women got entrance into the brahmanical community.... Many letters were published in the contemporary newspapers, ... in one such letter a writer declared that he could say with great confidence in himself that many of the wives, sons and grandsons- of many renowned Pandits were indeed sons and daughters of the Dhopā (washerman), Nāpit (barber), Mālī (flowerseller), Kumār (potter) etc. Having got entrance into many prosperous brahmins' houses, even the low caste women became pure brahmins' wives and naturally the food articles prepared by such wives came to be considered pure". "A letter published in the Darpan of 1833 was written by a woman. It becomes clear from the contents of the letter that she demanded such rights for women as to have education to mix freely with people, to select their own husbands, to be given in marriage at a proper time, to stop the selling of girls in auction, to stop giving in marriage to ones who had many wives, to allow the remarriage of the widows and so on".

The carreer and influence of Rājā Ram Mohan Roy may be regarded as the most important event in India of the 19th cent. A.D., which established a standard for social-cum-religious reform in different centres like Calcutta, Madras, Bombay and the Punjab. He may be called the first modern Indian who revolted against some of the existing practices of the Hindu society and who conceived of a renovated Indian society, built on both religious and social reform. His compaign, started in 1818, against the Satī System was successful in prohibiting it by a Government legislation. No less did Isvar Chandra Vidyasagar (1820-1891) contribute to the social reform in the shape of widow-remarriage and emancipation of Indian woman. English education and activities of Christian missionaries expedited to spread new ideas in different parts of India, specially when the Universities of Calcutta, Bombay and Madras were founded in 1857. The Brāhma Samāj, founded in 1824 became a refuge for many enlightened men in Bengal and also other parts of India. Keshab Chandra Sen and the teachings of Rāmakrishṇa and his followers brought about a revolution in religious life and their influence was felt in the making of a new society. In 1868 Sasipati Banerjee sponsored the remarriage of his widowed niece to a non-Brahmin and this was regarded as one of the "most violently radical that have as yet been performed among the most radical followers of Babu K.C. Sen."[2] Svāmi Dayānanda Saraswatī (1824-1883) in North India started a compaign against the Brahmin priesthood and social customs and founded the Ārya-samāj with the same mission of socio-religious reform in India. The leaders of nationalist movement were also involved in social reform and the British Government also encouraged them only to divert the attention of the people from political to social abuses. In 1890 Tilak, Ranade and some others advocated social reform in connection with marriage, viz., marriage-expenses, prohibition of polyandry, spread of female education, and a rise in the age of marriage of both the sexes.[3] But soon there was a split between the members, some were bent on only political reform and in Poona there was a possibility of riots on issues of reform. Surendranath Banerjee was a friend of social reform but his political ambition kept him away from social reform. Under the leadership of Gandhiji freedom in all spheres, political, social and economic came to be pursued as the programme of the National Movement.

However, local social reform movements were in full swing in Bombay, Madras and Bengal. Some of them formed caste reform associations, specially in Bombay. Bengal was the centre of Brāhma-samājists; and Ārya-samāj flourished in northern India. Sindh witnessed the rise of the Hindu Social Reform Association under the leadership of Dayaram Gidumal, which took some pledges like age-restriction and dowry etc. in marriage.

In 1905 Gokhale's Servants of India Society aimed at elevation of the depressed classes. In 1908 the National Social conference took a resolution for the gradual relaxation of caste-restrictions; and V.R. Sindhe and Chandavarkar wanted to do away with all Caste discriminations and to elevate the position of Pariahs. Thus the Social reform movement in the 20th cent. took a new turn when under the inspirations of M.K. Gandhi and B.R. Ambedkar attention was diverted to the breaking down of caste discriminations or even social equality.

In Madras also the Hindu Social Reform Association was started[5] by what Ranade called, "the Young Madras" - party in 1892. Annie Besant's 'Theosophical Society' also stimulated the task. Vivekananda's teachings spread more liberal ideas of social reform regarding castes, marriage and women. By the beginning of the 20th cent. was formed the Madras Hindu Social Reform Association which founded 'the Hindu Widows' Home' and which started the "Social purity movement". However, it can not be denied that the South India responded to the call of social reform later than the North India, on account of the rigidity of the caste system in South India.

In Bengal the Brāhmas abandoned more restrictions on social intercourse and specially on women's liberty than elsewhere in India. Among the Brāhmas, however, the leadership of Keshab

Sen in the sphere of social reform had a setback after his marriage alliance in 1878,[4] with the Coochbehar girl. Bengal paid more attention to political reforms. The Sādhāraṇ Brāhma Samāj, though breaking away from Keshab Sen tried to maintain the impulse of social reform under the leadership of Ānanda Mohan Bose. It started more schools for girls and the City College in Calcutta. Shibnath Sastri started in 1908 a Depressed-class Mission and worked among the tribal people in Bengal and Assam, who were drawn to Brāhmasamāj. Śaśipada Banerjee had already started a Widow's Home in 1887 in Calcutta for the first time in India, which, however, was run along orthodox lines and was rejected by the Sādhāraṇ Brāhma Samāj.

In the 20th cent., the Social Reform Movement in Bengal could not make any progress because the people's attention was diverted more towards nationalist movement. In some states like Mysore, Baroda and Travancore the Social Reform Movement gained more momentum in the early decades of the 20th cent. In 1909 the dedication of girls as devadāsi-s to temples was prohibited by legislation. The Mysore Government supported the State's institution the 'Ārya-dharmojjivanī Sabhā' in its attempt at marriage-reform and breakdown of caste-distinctions. In Baroda also in the same period laws were framed for social reforms like a Hindu Widow Remarriage Act in 1909, the Age of Consent Act in 1904 and a Civil Marriage Act in 1908, corresponding to the Brāhma Marriage Act.

Besides, by the end of the 19th cent. A.D. and the beginning of the 20th cent., were formed many caste associations in different parts of India which organised different caste conferences like the Kāyastha conference in 1887 and 1888, held at Lucknow and Allahabad respectively, which became the mainstay of the secular social reform movement. It may be pointed out that the Kāyastha communities did neither interdine nor intermarry. So these associations did their best to do away with all such inhibitions and to break down all caste distinctions among the Hindus. But a split soon took place among the Kāyasthas. The liberal group insisted on progressive acts like marriage reform, interdining and intermarriage among Kāyasthas at least and on temperance, as reflected in *Hindusthan Review* of Allahabad- (English Journal), but they were outvoted by the more conservative section. They, however, formed a Kāyastha Intermarriage Society in December, 1907 to promote mingling of Kāyasthas of different parts of India.

The Vaiśyas also established a conference in 1891 and though they were traders by profession, most of them did interdine but did not intermarry.[5] Even the Vaiśya Mahāsabhā of Baijnath could not go so far as to introduce widow-remarriage or intermarriage of sub-castes.

The Āryasamāj as a local social reform movement contributed no less than the Brāhma Samāj towards the uplift of the depressed classes and even of the tribal people. Gandhiji started preaching caste-reform ideas and in 1922 a section of the members of this institution under Bhai Paramanand, a Professor of the D.A.V. College of Lahore founded the Jat Pat Todak Mandal at Lahore with the mission of removal of all caste-discriminations within the samāj and in 1937 under the pressure of the Samājists the Ārya Marriage Validation Act (XIX of 1937) was passed by the Central Legislature to confirm the Legality of intercaste marriages among Āryas. It is interesting to note that like Dayananda, Vivekananda had thought in the earlier period that some social customs of the Hindus were not based on the true religious teaching of Hinduism and so they did not oppose the widow-Remarriage movement and the Age of consent Bill. They insisted on the education and liberation of women for the development of the nation.[6] Gandhiji, however, supported the varṇa system of four ideal classes as a natural division of society as satisfying "the religious, social and economic needs of a community" but he denounced the practices like untouchability. In the early 1920's he opposed interdining and inter-marriage between castes but in the early 1930's he took a neutral position on both. He could never accept the theory that true national unity could only be achieved by the complete removal of caste barriers to social intercourse.

The social reformers tried to enact a Civil Marriage Law in the early decades of this century by which a Hindu could marry any one belonging not to his own caste or religion. Two bills were raised in the Central Legislative Council in 1911 by Bhupendranath Basu and in 1918 by Vithalbhai Patel but not passed, until a bill drafted by Dr. Hari Singh Gour was passed, which amended the 1872 Special Marriage Act by eliminating the need of denying affiliation with established religious groups. Let us discuss, bye the by, the two castes, Kāyasthas and Vaidyas still holding prominent position in the society. The Karaṇa-s, originally scribes of the ancient period became merged in Kāyastha-s in medieval and modern India. Lokanātha has already been referred to as a Karaṇa and the Guṇaighar C.P. mentions a Karaṇa Kāyastha, i.e. a minister in charge of peace and war. We learn of a court-physician, author of *Śabdapradīpa* as belonging to a Karaṇa family, whose father and grandfather also had served in the same capacity two Pāla kings, Rāmapāla and Gobinda Chandra of Bengal. Sandhyākara Nandī, the famous poet and author of *Rāmacarita* speaks of his father as the leader of the karaṇa-s, and Minister of peace and war. The term 'Kāyastha' is noted in Viṣṇu and Yāj. smṛtis as a royal official and also in the inscriptions of 8th-11th cent. A.D. The Karaṇa and Kāyastha are also mentioned in *Rājataraṅginī*. The inscription of Amoghavarṣa[8] of 9th cent. A.D. refers to a Kāyastha caste of Western India. The inscriptions of later periods[9] also mention the Kāyasthas of North India.

According to Kulaji-s of Bengal the Kāyasthas are born of five attendants of five brahmins who came to Bengal, being invited by Ādiśūra. Dr. Bhandarkar thinks that the Kāyasthas were descended from Nagara Brāhmaṇa, settled in Bengal long before the 8th cent. A.D.[10] But R.C. Majumdar opines that "the evidence in support of a large scale immigration of Nagara brāhmaṇas is hardly convincing".[11] The *Rājataraṅginī*[12] refers to a brahmin Śivaratha who was a rouguish kāyastha and so strangulated in the reign of Jayasinha. From this we may infer that the term Kāyastha was still used in the sense of an officer in Kashmir of the 12th cent. A.D. and that the brāhmaṇa-s held such offices.

The Vaidya as a professional group of physicians is referred to in the Talamanchi plates[13] of Vikramāditya Cālukya, dated 660 A.D. and then in the South Indian records[14] of the 8th cent. A.D. R.C. Majumdar, however, thinks that "there is no definite reference to Vaidya as a caste in Bengal before the 12th cent. A.D.", obviously because the Karaṇa-s served as royal physicians in Vaṅga during the 11th-12th cent. A.D. and it is more likely that the Ambaṣṭhas of earlier days, noted as physicians in *Manusaṁhitā* came to be known as Vaidyas in later period. The Kulaji-s refer to Ādiśūra both as Ambaṣṭha and Vaidya and these mention the Sena kings as Vaidyas, though, of course, they contain little historical value.

Opinions differ as to the origin and position of the Kāyasthas, in earlier days and as reflected even in decisions of courts of modern India. The Calcutta High Court[15] (Bholanath Vs Emperor) held that they (of Bengal) were Śūdras and went so far as to hold that a Kāyastha could marry a Ḍom female. But the Privy Council[16] left undecided this issue in the case Asit Mohan vs-Nirode Mohan. The Allahabad and Patna High Courts held respectively in Tulsiram vs-Biharilal and in Isvari Prasad vs. Rai Hari Prasad that the Kāyasthas were dvijās and not śūdras.

The Vaidyas of Eastern India are at present divided generally into four types: Pañcakoṭi, Rāḍhi, Vaṅgaja and Vārendra. The Pañcakoṭi-s are again subdivided into two classes, Senabhūmi and Birbhūmi. The Vaidyas of Manbhum are said to belong to Senabhumi class. The Rāḍhiyas are also of three categories, of Śrīkhaṇḍa, Sātśaika and Saptagrām; and they use the surnames of Sena, Dāsa, Gupta, Deva, Kara etc. The Vaṅgajas differ little from the Rāḍhiyas and the Vaṅgajas are mainly of two branches, Senahāṭi and Chandanmahal, named after two important places of the district of Khulna. Vārendra Vaidyas are known as using the surnames of Nandin, Candra, Dhara, Kuṇḍa, Rakṣita, Dāsa, Datta, and Kara. It deserves mention that Vaidyas are little known in Assam except in two districts of Sylhet (now Bangladesh) and Kacchar. Pandit Umesh Chandra Dasgupta of the Vaidya community mentions the Assamese Bej-Baruas as Vaidyas in his

'Jāti-tattva-vāridhi' The intercaste marriage between Vaidyas and Kāyasthas at least in the eastern corner of Bengal is well-known to the sociologists. Pandit Dasgupta, the eminent Vaidya, admits in his book, noted above:- "The Kāyasthas with titles like Deva, Dāsa, Kara, Dhara, Datta, Soma, and Kuṇḍu were originally Vaidyas or Ambaṣṭhas but turned into Kāyastha-s when they took to the profession of the scribes". Bej-Barua is the title once offered to a family physician, a Brahmin or a Non Brahmin by the Kings of Ahom dynasty but now it is exclusively used by those who are known as brahmins in Assam. 'Bej' is obviously derived from 'Vaidya' and Barua from Vaṭu denoting a Brahmin, though of course, taken by some in the sense of a great man, recognised as such by the Ahom kings. However, like Vaidyas in Bengal, the Bej-Baruas are known in Assam as physicians. The intercaste marriage between Vaidyas and Brāhmaṇas in Assam is referred to in a letter from Sri B. Goswami to Mm. Kaviraj Gaṇapati Sen Saraswatī of Calcutta (Grey street).

The Kāyasthas are very rare in upper Assam and they are found to marry the daughters of the Kalitā-subcaste, as evidenced by the remarks of Mr. B.C. Allen, in the *Gazetteer of Lakhimpur* district:[18] "Kalitās who have risen above the necessity of manual labour frequently described themselves as Kāyastha-s" But the real Kāyasthas of the districts of Goalpara and Kamrup do never interdine or intermarry with the Kalitās. We find enough instances of intercaste marriage between two tribal groups of Kalitās and Kaots of Lakhimpur district and also among the subcastes known as Kumār-Kalitā, Saru Koch, Māli and Sonari in the same district. But in Ujani region of Assam the Kalitās are recognised as superior to Kaots and if any male member of the Kalitā group marries a female of the Kaots, he is to expiate himself by the penances of the Dharma texts. In Assam a lower class male is allowed to marry a higher class girl but a higher class male loses his caste, if he marries a lower class girl, as reflected in the observation of B.C. Allen, in *Lakhimpur district Gazetteer*:[19] "An unmarried girl who becomes pregnant does not forfeit her position in the society unless her lover is of lower caste". Elsewhere Mr.

Allen writes about the people of Lakhimpur district: "At the present day the Maomarias or the Maṭakas are cut off from communion with the other Vaiṣṇavas of Assam. Men of all castes are members of this sect but a Maṭak Brahmin, Kalitā or Ahom can not intermarry or eat with other Kalitās or Ahoms and the Maṭak members of each Brahmin caste form endogamous section in it."

In Assam the Brahmin priests of the Ḍom-s marry the daughters of the Ḍoms but they never offer their daughters to any Ḍom and they get them married with the grooms of their own castes. These ḍom-s are also known as 'Naḍiyal-s' and they live upon boating and fishing. B.C. Allen remarks: "The priests of these ḍom-s are said to be descended from a brahmin father and a naḍiyal mother but for all practical purposes they are naḍiyal-s and intermarry with naḍiyal girls".[20] It is interesting to note that the ancestors of the people belonging to Kachari-caste came from China in the 11th cent. A.D. and planted colonies in Assam. The Kacharis of upper Assam are known as 'Rājavaṁśi-s and the Hindus. Many Khens of Kamrup are intermarried with Kalitās, Kochs and Rājavaṁśi-s. The Kalitā-s were originally Buddhists, as noted in *"Indian Village Community"* of H.B. Baden Powel[21] (published in 1897) and many Kalitās are now known as Kāyastha-s (*Lakhimpur district Gazetteer*).[22]

Sri Prabhat Chandra Barua, descendant of Rājā Bulchand Barua, known as Kāyastha of the Dāsa family of Rāṅgamāṭi of Dhubri area was recognised as leader of the society by the Brahmins and Kāyastha-s of Goalpara district in 1309 B.S., He got his brother Sri Ramakrishna Barua married with a daughter of the Mitra family of South Rāḍh at Bagbazar, Calcutta in 1314 B.S. His son Pramathesh Chandra was also married with the daughter of Sri Birendra Nath Mitra of the same Kāyastha family of South Rāḍh in 1329 B.S. The Zemindars of Mechpara and Parvatjoyar estate used to get their sons and daughters married with persons of different castes; and such marriages were accepted only as 'union of sexes'. Such intercaste marriage is also heard of in South India in cases like that of Lakṣmī Devī, daughter of the pure Brahmin Rajagopalachariya, married with the son of Gandhiji, a gandhavaṇik i.e., a Vaiśya. Sm. Vijayalakṣhmī, daughter of the Kashmiri Brahmin Motilal Nehru was married with the Vaiśya Hatilal. Sarojinī, daughter of brahmin Aghore Chatterjee was married with the Śūdra Mr. Naidu. Such connections may also be taken not as marriage but mere union of sexes. W.W. Hunter tells us in his "Dacca Blue Book", published in 1868[23] that "the Syhlet Sahoos claim to rank with or immediate below the Kaistas to whom they give daughter in marriage", and Gopal Chandra Sastri mentions in "Hindu Law"[24] that "in Eastern districts such as Syhlet and Tippera there is a custom of intermarriage between the Kāyasthas and the Sahoos". One of the brilliant scholars of the Medhai family of the Sahoos of the village of Maryatkandi of the Karimgunj subdivision, named Bepin Chandra Das married a learned Brahmin daughter of Poona named Ramabai Sarasvatī by Act-3 of 1872, to be explained later on.

REFERENCES

1. J.N. Banerjee. *The Alumni Association*, (Dept. of A.I.H. & C., C.U., 1960), pp. 273 f.
2. *Social Reform in Bengal* (by Sitanath Tattvabhusan), pp. 88-89.
3. Govt. of Bombay, *Source material for a history of the Freedom movement in India*, II, p. 201.
4. *The Brāhma Samāj*, by M.C. Parekh, pp. 100 f and 211.
5. Baijnath in Chintamani, *Indian Scoial Reform*, (Madras, 1901) I, 159.
6. Vivekananda's *"Speeches and writings"*, pp. 748-749.
7. Vide M.V. Shah, *"Social Philosophy of Gandhiji"*, pp. 6-67.
8. *E.I.*, XVIII, 251.
9. *E.I.*, XII, 46 & 61; *Proc. A.S.B.*, 1880, p. 78; *E.I.*, XIX, 50.
10. *I.A.*, LXI, 48.
11. *H.B.*, p. 435.
12. VIII, 131.
13. *E.I.*, IX, 102.

14. *E.I.*, XVII, 291-309; *I.A.*, 1893, p. 57 f; *E.I.*, VIII, 317-321.
15. *I.L.R.*, 51 Cal- 488.
16. *L.R.*, 47. *IA*, 140-145.
17. *Vaidya-Hitaiṣiṇī*, No. 1, p. 3.
18. Vol. VIII, p. 117.
19. Vol. III, p. 117.
20. *Assam Dist. Gaz.*, vol. viii, p. 121.
21. pp. 134-135.
22. VIII, p.117.
23. p. 284.
24. Pub. 1902 by B. Banerjee & Co. p. 75.

CHAPTER - VIII

Legislation in India

Now let us turn our attention to the Laws regarding marriage passed during the period of British rule in India and also in the post-independence period.

To begin with, marriage was taken up as a matter under the jurisdiction of the Lawcourts, it lost its original character as a sacrament and thus as an indissoluble tie and it came to be regarded as nothing but a mere contract, "an alliance between a man and a woman recognised by law".[1] Traditionally marriage among the Hindus was and is still conceived to be a religious rite in which the girl is but an object of gift by the father to the husband by a ceremonial. But the courts hold that no ceremony is required for the completion of a marriage.[2] The performance of the ceremony saptapadī or seven steps is, however, required for the completion of a valid marriage.[3] The court holds that marriages among many castes are performed even without it and they are completed if any other form by any caste usage is followed. "Thus in view of law, ceremony was but a mere evidence of marriage."[4]

The Britishers did nothing to disturb the private law of the Indian community in the administration of law and justice. The laws and usages of different communities were respected as evidenced by the Regulation 1 of 1781 of which section 27 provided that "in all suits regarding inheritance, marriage, caste and other religious usages or institutions the laws of the Koran with respect to Muhammedans and those of the śāstras with respect to Gentus, shall be invariably adhered to". The complaint of the judges of the Supreme Court of Calcutta regarding "the chaotic confusion in the state of law they had to administer" led subsequently "to the appointment of Indian Law Commission" under the Charter Act of 1833 with Lord Macaulay as the head. Thus were evolved the first codes of Civil and criminal procedure in 1859 and 1860-61 respectively.

'The Caste Disabilities Removal Act' was passed in 1850 which did away with the traditional Hindu theory that loss of one's caste due to some lapses in following the traditional ideas of morality was to be penalised even by forfeiture of inheritance (Cf. Mita. II.140 showing an outcaste and his issue losing the right of inheritance). At the initiative of the British Judges the Act was passed in 1850, known as the Caste Disabilities Removal Act declaring that "no loss of caste shall involve forfeiture of any right to property in the entire British India". Another historic Act of 'Hindu Widows Remarriage, 1856' was passed which amended the Hindu law to no mean degree, removing all obstacles to the marriage of Hindu widows.

The orthodox Hindu marriage law was subordinated to legislature much more in 1866 when was passed 'the Native Converts' Marriage Dissolution Act' which provided that if in consequence of a party's conversion to christianity, the other party repudiates or deserts the other for the space of six continuous months a divorce might be granted.The party converted to christianity must sue the other for conjugal society[5] and the Court could dissolve the marriage, if the respondent refused to cohabit for a period of one year. This Act granted divorce only in case of one's conversion to christianity and of desertion on this ground alone.

Next the Civil Marriage Act,[6] 1872 which extends to the whole of India except the States of Jammu and Kashmir provides a form of marriage for persons "neither of whom professes the christian or the Jewish, or the Hindu or the Muhammaden or the Parsi or the Buddhist or the Sikh or the Jaina religion, or between persons each of whom professes one or other of the following religions, that is to say, the Hindu, Buddhist, Sikh or Jaina religion, upon the following conditions:

(1) neither party must, at the time of marriage have a husband or wife living;

(2) The man must have completed his age of 18 years and the woman her age of 14 years;

(3) each party must, if he or she has not completed the age of 21 years, have obtained the consent of his or her father or guardian to the marriage; and

(4) the parties must not be related to each in any degree of consanguinity or affinity which according to any law to which-either of them is subject, renders a marriage between them illegal.

It is to be noted that no law or custom, other than one relating to consanguinity or affinity shall prevent them from marrying. This Act enjoins that "the marriage shall be solemnised in the presence of the Registrar and of three witnesses who signed the declaration", in the form stating that "I (A) take thee (B) to be my lawful wife (or husband)". It is interesting to note the most important conditions of the validity of a marriage by this Act, noted above (1-4) and particularly that neither he nor she belonged to any religion (or religious caste).

The Anand Marriage Act[7] was passed to remove doubts as to the validity of the marriage ceremony common among the Sikhs called Anand. All marriages, solemnised according to the Sikh marriage ceremony called Anand would be deemed valid in law, of course, with exemption of certain marriages from Act (a) any marriage betwen persons not professing the Sikh religion or any marriage, judicially declared to be null and void. Marriages within prohibited degrees are also taken to be invalid.

The Amendment Act[8] was passed to do away with the difficulty arising out of the Act of 1872 by which the parties of the marriage had to declare that they belonged to no religion or caste.

The Baroda Tyranny Removal Act[9] ensured actions to be taken against the caste-council in case they did excommunicate any member of the caste for any caste offence including breach of endogamy.

The Ārya Samāja Marriage Validation Act[10] was passed to legalise intercaste marriages among the Āryasamājits in India (except Part B States). Next was passed Hindu Mariage Disabilities Removal Act[11] extending to the whole of India except Part B States legalising a marriage between Hindus, belonging to the same Gotra or Pravara and to different subdivisions of the same caste. Intermarriage between different castes and subcastes and between Hindu, Sikh and Jain has been legalised by Act XXX of 1949 Hindu Marriages Validity Act. The anuloma and pratiloma marriages were held valid according to religious texts, as analysed before. But a practice has grown up that intermarriage between different subdivisions of the same Varṇa or tribe does not now take place. For instance, there is no connubium between the Varendra, the Rāḍha and Vaidīka subdivisions of the Bengal brahmins nor between the Bangaja, Uttara-Rādhiya, the Vārendra and the Dakṣiṇa-Rādhīya Kāyasthas of Bengal. In Oudh also marriages between subdivisions of Kāyasthas are not in practice. In the Madras case of Inderun V. Ramaswamy the Privy council upheld an intermarriage between two different subdivisions of the Śūdra tribe. Custom of intercaste marriage is found in Sylhet and Tippera districts, as between Vaidyas and Kāyasthas as well as between Kāyasthas and Sahoos. So in Bombay Presidency a marriage between different sects of the Liṅgāyats is not held invalid.[12] Even a woman, converted to Hinduism can by this Act marry a Hindu.[13]

The Bombay Prevention of Hindu Bigamous Marriages Act, 1946[14] provides for the prevention of bigamous marriages among the Hindus. The term Hindu here includes a Sikh, a Jain, a Buddhist, a follower of the Ārya or Brāhma Samāj or a convert to Hinduism. Bigamous marriage means the marriage of a person during the lifetime of his or her spouse, if the marriage of such person with such spouse has not been dissolved or declared void by a court, or is not void according to the custom of the community he or she belongs to. Penalty prescribed for solemnising bigamous marriage is imprisonment upto 6 months or fine or both. The Bombay Hindu Divorce Act[15] provides for a right of divorce among all communities of Hindus in certain circumstances like impotency, lunacy, leprosy, desecration by the defendant for a continuous period of 4 yrs. and cases where the defendant has not been heard of as being alive for 7 years, and the defendant, if a husband has any other woman as a concubine or if a wife, a concubine of any other man or leading the life of a prostitute. Some such laws were passed in Madras in 1947 and in Madhya Pradesh in 1955. The Madras Nambudri Act of 1933 also enacted the prevention of bigamy unless in cases of leprosy, of being outcaste and want of a male child.

The Special Marriage Act (No.43)[16] provides a special form of marriage in certain cases, for the registration of such and some other marriages and for divorce. "It extends to the whole of India except the State of Jammu and Kashmir and applies also to citizens of India domiciled in the territories to which this Act extends who are outside the said territories". By this Act "a marriage between any two persons may be solemnised under the following conditions:

(a) neither party has a spouse living;

(b) neither party is an idiot or a lunatic;

(c) the male has completed the age of 21 years and the female that of 18 years.

(d) the parties are not within the degrees of prohibited relationship, provided that where a custom permits such marriage, such marriage may be solemnised, notwithstanding that they are within the degrees of prohibited relationship".

It is worth noting that "the parties to such marriage shall give notice in writing to the marriage officer of the district in which at least one of the parties to the marriage, has resided at least for the period of not less than thirty days immediately preceding the date of submitting such notice". "The marriage solemnised under this Act of any member of an undivided family who professes the Hindu, Buddhist, Sikh or Jaina religion shall be deemed to effect his severence from such family". However, "subject to provisions of section 19 rights and disabilities in regard to the right of succession to any property as a person to whom the cases of Disabilities Removal Act, 1850 applies", are not affected by this Act. This Act also offers power to the court to decree restitution of conjugal rights and judicial separation, if the court is satisfied with the truth of the statements, made by the aggrieved party, husband or wife, in the petition concerned. It also provides for nullity of marriage and divorce under certain conditions.[17]

"Any marriage solemnised under this Act shall be voidable and may be annulled by a decree of nullity, if -

(i) the marriage has not been consummated owing to the wilful refusal of the respondent to consummate the marriage, or

(ii) the respondent was at the time of the marriage pregnant by some person other than the petitioner, or

(iii) the consent of either party to the marriage was obtained by coercion or fraud, as defined in the Indian Contract Act, 1872 (9 of 1872). (1) Notwithstanding that a marriage is null and void under section 24, any child of such marriage who would have been legitimate if the marriage had been valid shall be legitimate". (2) Where a decree of nullity is granted in respect of a voidable marriage under section 25, any child begotten or conceived before the decree is made ... shall be deemed to be their legitimate child not-with-standing the decree of nullity. It is intresting to note the comment here that "the child of void and voidable marriage shall be legitimate".

Sec. 27 permits a petition for divorce to "be presented to the District Court either by the husband or the wife on the ground that the respondent - (a) has, after the solemnisation of the marriage had voluntary sexual intercourse with any person other than his or her spouse; or (b) has deserted the petitioner for a continuous period of not less than two years immediately preceding the presentation of the petition; or (c) is undergoing a sentence of imprisonment for seven years or more for an offence as defined in I.P.C. (45 of 1860); or (d) has since the solemnisation of the marriage treated the petitioner with cruelity; or (e) has been incurably of unsound mind or has been suffering continuously or intermittently from mental disorder....". A wife may also present a petition for divorce to the District Court on the ground - (i) that her husband has, since the solemnisation of the marriage, been guilty of rape, sodomy or bestiality; (ii) that a decree or order has been passed against the husband awarding maintenance to the wife notwithstanding that she was living apart and that since the passing of such decree or order, cohabitation between the parties has not been resumed for one year or upwards.This Act (Sec 28) permits also 'divorce by mutual consent' - (i) a petition of divorce may be presented to the District Court by both the parties together on the ground that they have been living separately for a period of one year or more, that they have not been able to live together and that they have mutually agreed that the marriage should be dissolved; and (ii) on the motion of both the parties ... the District Court shall, on being satisfied after hearing the parties ... pass a decree declaring the marriage to be dissolved with effect from the date of the decree. By Sec. 30 of this Act after "the marriage has been dissolved by a decree of divorce, either party to the marriage may marry again". This Act (Sec. 43) distinctly mentions "penalty on married person marrying again under this Act". "Every person who being at the time of marriage procures a marriage of himself or herself to be solemnised under this Act shall be deemed to have committed an offence under Sec. 494 or Sec 495 of I.P.C. (45 of 1860) as the case may be and the marriage so solemnised shall be void".

Last was passed the Hindu Marriage Act[18] in 1955 (The word 'Hindu' under the Act, 1955 includes a Buddhist, a Jaina or Sikh by religion and any person who is not a Muslim, Christian, Parsi or Jew. Thus this Act does not only codify the Hindu law of marriage or divorce but it has brought about remarkable changes. It permits not only intercaste marriage but allows marriage between a Hindu, a Jaina, a Sikh and a Buddhist) on 18th May, which brought about some substantial and far-reaching changes in the Hindu law of marriage. So long Hindu marriage was regarded as a sort of sacrament and not at all a mere contract between the parties. But this Act has stripped Hindu marriage of its character as a sacrament and has invested it with the characteristics of contractual relationship between the parties. Divorce may now be granted by its section 13 and a decree of nullity of marriage may be had under sections 11 and 12 of this Act. Besides, by this Act a marriage between a Hindu, Buddhist, a Jain or a Sikh by religion is also held valid, if solemnised under this Act, and monogamy has been made compulsory.[19] Marriage is subject to registration under section 8 of this Act and this law deals with the rights and liabilities of the parties bound by marriage.

This law is, like the Special Marriage Act of 1954, applicable to all citizens of India barring the State of Jammu and Kashmir and to all Hindus living in India and abroad. It lays down almost the same conditions under which a marriage may be solemnised. It is less strict in the sense that "the bridegroom must complete the age of 18 years and the bride that of 15 years at the time of marriage". But it insists that "where the bride has not completed 18 years, the consent of her guardian", if any, is required (Sec. 5). It lays down that the State Government may frame rules and arrange the registration of such marriage (Sec. 8).

This Act (Sec 13), like Special Marriage Act of 1954 provides for the dissolution of marriage on petition of the husband or the wife, by a decree of divorce on the ground that the other party -

(i) is living in adultery, or

(ii) has ceased to be a Hindu by conversion to another religion, or

(iii) has been incurably of unsonund mind for at least three years, or

(iv) has been suffering from incurable leprosy for at least three years, or

(v) has been suffering from venereal disease for at least 3 years, or

(vi) has renounced the world by entering any religious order, or

(vii) has not been heard of as living for 7 years or more, or

(viii) has not resumed cohabitation for a period of 2 years or upwards after the passing of a decree for judicial separation against the respondent, or

(ix) has failed to comply with a decree for restitution of conjugal rights for a period of 2 years or upwords after the passing of the decree".

"A wife may also present a petition for divorce on the grounds:

(i) in the case of any marriage solemnised before the commencement of this Act, that the husband had married again before such commencement or that any other wife of the husband married before such commencement was alive at the time of the solemnisation of the marriage of the petitioner, provided that in the either case the other wife is alive at the time of the presentation of the petition; or

(ii) that the husband has, since the solemnisation of the marriage, been guilty of rape, sodomy or bestiality".

Thus this Act marks a great departure from the traditional position of the ancient Hindu marriage. Hindu marriage in ancient India did not admit of any divorce (In recent times we come across a relatively high rate of divorce in our Indian society, obviously under the western influence, which may be taken as a concomitant of modern urbanisation and individualism and strict control of sexual relations outside marriage) or dissolution of marriage but this Act allows divorce or dissolution on certain conditions, noted above and thus Hindu marriage is noted as turned into a contractual relationship between the parties. It is interesting to note that this Act was passed in the Parliament of Free India on the initiative of Dr. Ambedkar, the then law-minister in the teeth of serious opposition from the conservative section of the people of India. The fundamental change by this Act is that caste distinctions have been abolished altogether. The word 'Hindu' of this Act does not refer to any caste but it includes a Buddhist, a Jain, a Sikh, even a Vīraśaiva, a Liṅgāyat and a follower of the Brāhma, Prārthanā or Ārya-samāj, thus obliterating all distinctions between caste, creed or sect at present prevailing in the Hindu society. This Act does not prescribe any ceremony as an essential condition of Hindu marriage. Nothing is more well calculated to do away with all barriers of castes or sects. It encourages young persons to marry any one of their choice, that is, mutual contract and love marriage. However, it is expected to be a potent instrument in the integration of Hindu community.

This Act (Sec 14) does not allow any court to entertain any petition for dissolution of a marriage by a decree of divorce unless besides the conditions, noted above, "three years have elapsed since the date of marriage", except in cases of "exceptional hardship to the petitioner or of exceptional depravity on the part of the respondent". The interests of children were safeguarded by this Act and the husband was required to pay to the wife for her maintenance and support, in case she remains chaste and unmarried, either at a time, or in monthly instalments so long as she lives. The court shall consider "whether there is a reasonable possibility of a reconcilation between the parties before the expiration of the said three years". Besides, this Act does not allow "the second marriage until one year has elapsed since the decrees of diverce or the disposal of the appeal thereof". Thus this Act is very careful to look to the interests of both the parties concerned with marriage, granting freedom to both of them as far as possible. This Act disallowed bigamy, as noted above, like the Saurāṣṭra Prevention of the Hindu Bigamous Marriages Act of 1954 and similar Act, passed by the Madhya Pradesh Government in 1955 declaring all bigamous marriages as nullified and liable to punishment under section 494 of the Indian Penal Code.

Now let us consider some salient features of this Act. This Act "applies to any person who is a Hindu by religion in any of its forms, who is a Buddhist, a Jaina or Sikh by religion and to any other person domiciled in the territories to which this Act expands who is not a Muslim, a Christian, Parsi or Jew by religion, unless it is proved that any such person would not have been governed by the Hindu Law or by any custom or usage as part of that law in respect of any of the matters dealt with herein if this Act had not been passed". (Sec. 2). The term 'Hindu' of this Act means also "a person who, though not a Hindu by religion is nevertheless, a person to whom this Act applies by virtue of the provisions contained in this section". The terms 'Custom' and 'usage' of this Act signify any rule which having been continuously and uniformly observed for a long time, has obtained the force of law among Hindus in any local area, tribe, community, group or family".

This Act explains "full blood" and 'half blood' as 'two persons related to each other by 'full blood' when they are descended from a common ancestor by the same wife and by 'half blood' when they are descended from a common ancestor but by different wives; and "uterineblood" as two persons when they are descended from a common ancestress but by different husbands". It explains 'sapiṇḍa' relationship as referring to any person extending as far as the third generation (inclusive) in the line of ascent through the mother, and the fifth (inclusive) in the line of ascent through the father. "Two persons are said to be 'Sapiṇḍa's of each other if one is a lineal ascendant of the other within the limits of sapiṇḍa-relationship, or if they have a common lineal ascendant who is within the limits of sapiṇḍa relationship with reference to each of them". Two persons are said to be within the 'degrees of prohibited relationship' - (i) if one is a lineal ascendant of the other; or (ii) if one was the wife or husband of a lineal ascendant or descendant of the other; or (iii) if one was the wife of the brother or of the father's or mother's brother or of the grandfather's or grandmother's brother of the other; or (iv) if the two are brother and sister, uncle and niece, aunt and nephew, or children of brother and sister or of two brothers or of two sister'. (Cf. Sec. 3)

In a case on custom of sagotra marriages which is also sanctioned by this Act repealing the Hindu Marriage Disabilities

Removal Act of 1946 that validated Sagotra marriages it was held that it must be proved that the usage had been accepted in practice for a long period. (Madhavrao V Raghavendra - 18 Bom. L.R. 196). This Act validates marriage between persons related to each other within the prohibited degree of Sapiṇḍa relationship, if that marriage is sanctioned by custom [Sub-Sec (a)]. Such marriage is very common in South India, sp. Madras.

It has already been noted that this All-India Act (H.M. Act, '55) prevents bigamy among the Hindus and it has introduced monogamy. No question of polygamy. Bigamy is now an offence, punishable under Sec. 17, the scope of Sections 494 and 495 being extended to the Hindus. States like Bombay, Madras, Madhya Pradesh and Saurāṣṭra passed laws for prevention of bigamy like that of Bombay in 1946, that of Madras in 1946, that of Madhya Pradesh in 1955 and that of Saurāṣṭra in 1955. These are repeated by this Central Act. In Sec. 6 this Act mentions clearly the names of guardians for the consent in marriage for the bride. In Sec. 7 it refers to ceremonies like Saptapadīgamana for the completion of Hindu marriage. But "any irregularity in observance of ceremonies will not be a ground for declaring a Hindu marriage void or voidable under sec. 11 and 12 of this Act." The Sec. 13 of this Act gives us details of divorce, in Hindu marriage as noted before, for different reasons. It is worth noting that this Act does not permit any court to entertain any petition for dissolution of marriage by a decree of divorce within three years of marriage. It has already been mentioned that this Act enacts punishment of bigamy. The first condition of a legal Hindu marriage (Sec 5) is that "neither of the party will have a spouse living". Sec. 11 prescribes the marriage, made otherwise to be void and this section extends the scope of section 494 and 495 of I.P.C.

We must not miss to mention another Act No XIX of 1946 (23rd April) "to give Hindu married women a right to separate residence and maintenance under certain circumstances". Sec 2 of this Act mentions the following grounds like (i) if her husband is suffering from anv loath some disease, (ii) if he is guilty of such crulety, intolerable to her, (iii) if he is guilty of desecration, (iv) if he marries again, (v) if he ceases to be a Hindu by conversion to another religion, (vi) if he keeps a concubine, and (vii) for any other justifiable cause. Ofcourse, she would have this benefit, "if she is unchaste or ceases to be a Hindu by conversion to another religion".

However, from the above survey we learn that a Hindu husband can not remarry unless he lawfully dissolves his first wife. Anyone doing so is liable to punishment under sec.494 of I.P.C., noted before. Some think that the State is authorised "to secure for all citizens a uniform civil code throughout the territory of India"; and that such a code would help us with step towards national consolidation. To check the abuse of religion the Supreme Court calls for a uniform civil code, (Cf. the *Stateman*, 11.5.95) which is expected to prevent injustice towards women. We may remember the Supreme Court judgement in the Shah Bano case and also the observations of Dr. B.R. Ambedkar on the need of such a common civil code in the country, which would be voluntary in nature. Some apprehend that the Governments have so long failed to enact a uniform civil code for fear of losing votes of minority communities. However, the progressive people, irrespective of political parties of India would hail this historic achievement.

We may quote Jawaharlal Nehru's remark in this connection: "In my opinion everyone in India should marry outside his or her community".[20] He believed that "marriage should be based on a complete understanding, a perfect union of minds,"[21] and it should take place between two individuals by mutual agreement. When in 1942 his daughter Indira (our most popular Late Prime-Minister of modern India) announced her desire to marry Feroze Gandhi, a Parsee youngman, there was some criticism among the orthodox section of the society. But Nehru issued a press statement: "A marriage is a personal and domestic matter, affecting chiefly the two parties concerned and partly their families. Though parents may and should advise in the matter, the choice or ultimate decision must be with the two parties concerned". Nehru's sister and some of his cousins were also married out to their community.

It is interesting to point out that the Britishers remained indifferent to social customs of the Indians as regards marriage, adoption, partition and inheritance because they took lessons from the history of the Muslim rule that some Muhammeden rulers interferred with the social and religious life of the Hindus only to invite their ruin. The Indians were left to live in the cobweb of their own social superstitions, because they knew that the social emancipation of the Indians meant the end of the foreign rule in India. But we have analysed before how the Indians had fought for political and social reform in the 19th and 20th centuries. The Britishers, however, passed some laws regulating the social life of the Hindus, not jeopardising their own interests, as for instance, the Caste Disabilities Removal Act of 1850, mentioned before. But in post-independence period the laws, as analysed above, have been passed with respect to marriage, to extend more freedom to persons of both sexes and of different sects or creeds. But the people are not yet sufficiently educated to change their attitude to life and society and hence freedom, so granted has often been misused. The success of social legislation depends on a better or wider system of education among the masses. But unfortunately the rate of literacy among the people of free India is still so poor. The Government of India, has however, paid greater attention to education of our land and let us hope for a brighter future. Thanks to the State Government of W. Bengal for the works of development of the country and for the spread of literacy among the masses. We have already noticed that the Hindus have rules, both endogamous and exogamous in matters of marriage. The Hindus are now divided into a number of castes which are endogamous groups, but in practice each caste is again subdivided into a number of sub-castes, each sub-caste into a number of sections. These sections are again divided into subsections as vīśā or daśa in terms of locality. For example, we may cite such sub-divisions among the Vaiśyas, as pointed out by Kapadia[23]: "There is a caste called Vania... divided into subcastes lād, maḍh, poravād, nāgar, śrīmāli etc. The lād is divided into sections, Vīśā and dāśa and the vīśā is again demarcated as Ahmedabadi, Khambhati etc according to the locality of habitation". Even at present when legislation is in favour of intercaste marriage, breaches of caste endogamy are liable to excommunication from the caste. An individual excommunicated is refused cooperation of the members of his caste in cases of marriage and funeral ceremonies when the need of cooperation is actively felt. The Hindus are so much caste-minded that mere legislation will not break the ice.

The majority of young graduates are willing to get their children in marriage outside their own castes. This is indeed a healthy sign of materialisation of the idea of a classless society in near future. There is no denying the fact that modern industrial organisation has brought about major changes in the castesystem - (i) freedom in one's occupation and (ii) people flock to towns or cities. Eating in hotels and railway travel are major factors mitigating caste distinction in matter of food and drink and in increasing social intercourse among members of different castes. But even in cities like Calcutta the weakening of such restrictions has not totally led to the disruption of caste hierarchy. Rather many castes have built their own residential buildings and established charitable institutions for the welfare of the members of a particular caste; and they publish their journals for focussing their importance. Sometimes picnics and annual social gatherings are arranged castewise.

Opportunities to both the sexes to mix together in coeducational institutions and in mixed clubs and to work together in offices and institutions are the most important factors to accelerate the tempo of intercaste marriage in our present society. Co-education is preferred by those who support the idea of intercaste marriage but the establishment of separate institutions for girls proves the prejudices and apprehensions of the Hindu society towards co-education. Besides, mixed clubs and annual socials are found to be organised also castewise.

We have already noted that the exogamy of the Hindus of both Sapiṇḍa and Gotra prohibits marriage between members of the same gotra, and those related to each other within certain generations on the father's and mother's side. Gotra, however, ceased to be a family group from the Sūtra period when it became linked with the Pravara indicating a school of ritual or learning to which one belonged. In Bombay State the restriction of gotra on marriage was removed by the Hindu Marriage Disabilities Removal Act. The Hindu marriage Act of 1955, as noted before, does away with the endogamous restriction of caste and exogamous restriction of gotra.

Now let us throw some light on the joint family in India to show how it has been hard hit by the system of intercaste marriage, specially in modern Indian society. Karve defines joint family as "a group of people who generally live under one roof, who eat food cooked at one hearth, who hold property in common and who participate in common worship and are related to each other as some particular type of kindred". Its chief features are (i) large size, (ii) joint property, (iii) common house, (iv) cooperative organisation, (v) common religion, (vi) a producive unit, and (vii) mutual rights and obligations. The Aryans settled down in ancient period in different parts of the world and joint family had come into being in ancient India, as in ancient Roman society.

This system has some merits of its own like ensuring economic progress, division of labour among the members of the family, opportunity of leisure, social insurance for each child, young and old and developing social virtues like sacrifice, selflessness, mutual love and affection. Some scholar thinks that it fosters the spirit of socialism. It is a corporation where father is the main trustee. But it has been highly denounced for some defects like home for idlers, hindrance in the development of personality, encouraging litigation and leading to quarrels. It denies privacy to newly married couples. Hence in modern times it is rapidly breaking in cities and it exists still today to a certain extent only in villages among the agricultural families. We have already pointed out some factors leading to its disintegration like industrialisation which forces people to move to new places of factories, decline of agriculture and village trades as a result of which village craftsmen fail to compete in quality or price with those, produced in newly established factories. Western influence on the life of modern India, new outlook and ideology, specially relating to marriage and divorce is highly responsible for breakdown of joint-family. We have treated modern legislation like Civil Marriage Act of 1872, Hindu Marriage Act of 1954 and 1955 and Hindu Succession Act of 1956 and other Laws on regulating marriage, noted above, passed in different parts of India. Adult boys and girls are now free to marry according to their own choice. Women are given much more liberty in settling marriage and in cases of divorce under certain conditions. The Hindu Succession Act offers equal rights of inheritance to women as well. K.S . Sambasivan (Working Class Families in Alagappa Textiles - *Indian Journal of Social Work*, 1946-47, vol. II, p. 134) thinks that industrialisation is mainly responsible for the breakdown of joint-family system. The workers in mills and factories are said to have expressed their views in favour of separate (and not-joint) families. However, to judge impartially, joint-family system does not always crush the spirit of individuality, rather it is a corporate institution where each member of the joint-family can enjoy many facilities, if one can follow the path of compromise and mutual adjustment and if one does one's duty under the loving guardianship of superior members of the family.

The prominent features of modern family may be pointed out here to show the effects of intercaste marriage in our society. Marriage in traditional families was contracted by parents, but now it is, specially in cases of intercaste marriage, settled by the partners, as an ultimate result of courtship or falling in love. Woman is no longer the devotee of man but an equal partner in life with equal rights. Women at present, in different strata of our society are economically independent, both husband and wife being engaged outside home in earning. Marriage is now a matter of contract, hence no question of performance of religious rites, as performed in traditional systems. The use of contraception has lowered the rate of birth of children. As a result the size of the family is much smaller, and the modern family is in face of instability. Marriage-bonds are weakened. The old ideal of fidelity in sex-relationship is highly affected. The members of the same family are formed to be engaged in different pursuits of life. The modern rule of marriage is more materialistic and self-centred. Frankly speaking, marriage is no longer a religious segment but a temporary contract, meant for sexual gratification and companionship.

In spite of all such defects creeping in modern society marriage in all circumstances presents as an essential institution of our family. We should try our best to arrange better marriages. Marriages, specially intercaste ones are often the outcome of romantic love and not of well-calculated thoughts; and so sometimes they end in sad cases of divorce. In all cases of marriage mental adjustment between partners should or must be insisted on and the family must be built on a democratic basis. Bogardus (Sociology, p. 105) speaks of a democratic family as "one in which the husband and wife share the authority more or less equally and according to a prearranged division of labour. It is a group whose life is based not primarily on the fear and force of authority but on the drawing power of mutual respect and affection (Rational love rules)". The main function of a family is procreating and rearing children in which both the partners are equally interested and hence it is the duty of the State to regulate family-life by strict regulation, already noted before. At present the State helps the married couple with services of public welfare like those of marriage guidance bureaus and family relations clinics and of child-welfare centres.

The caste system has been prevailing in India from very ancient times, as discussed before. It has both merits and demerits. Where caste is determined by one's birth, one can not alter it by one's individual action except in rare cases like Viśvāmitra. Unless caste-barriers are broken, mutual distrust among people of different castes will persist and that is why the Government of India intends to do away with castes and build a caste or classless society in India. The reformist movement, analysed before, has practically tried to cut the root of caste-system by spread of western education. We must not miss to mention Jyotirao Phooley who was a Māli by caste, little educated. He started the 'Satyaśodhaka samāja' in Pune in 1873 for exhibiting one's worth, irrespective of caste.

The Constitution of India asserts in its preamble that India is a secular Democratic Republic where all citizens, irrespective of castes would be provided with justice and equal opportunity-social, economic and political; and that is possible only in a society where there are no distinctions of classes or castes. The right of equality to all citizens is guaranteed in section 15 and 16 of the Constitution where all barriers on grounds of religion, race, caste, sex, place of birth or any of them are done away with. Article 17 has abolished untouchability and Article 19 has given the right of freedom about one's lawful profession. The Article 46 provides the weaker section of the people, particularly the Scheduled castes and Scheduled tribes with all facilities and it "shall protect them from social injustice and all forms of exploitation". Various schemes are already worked upon to uplift their status — social and economic.

The rigidity of castesystem is softened to a large extent but it still perists at least in village-areas. In cases of intercaste marriage, specially of love-marriages young people are ready to break through the caste. Even in political circles the elections in India are contested sometimes on the basis of castesystem. Voters are much influenced to vote for their caste-candidates. Political leaders maintain their casteism even after the election is over. To speak the truth, Indian democracy has in practice encouraged castesystem. Atrocities on Harijans prove the failure of the Government to check casteism. The latest judgement of the Supreme Court on the Mondal case shows the strength of the casteism still flourishing in India, in spite of all efforts to remove the evils of casteism. However, the spread of education in India would strengthen the young people to transcend all castebarriers; and intercaste marriage, we may hope, would usher in an age when people would give up caste-consciousness and meet together to build a new India.

REFERENCES

1. Hindu Code, p. 223.
2. 30 *Bombay Indian Law Reports*, p. 197.
3. 12 *Calcutta Ind. Law Reports*, pp. 140-143.
4. Hindu Code, p. 260.
5. Section - 4 and 5.
6. Act No. III of 1872.
7. (1909).
8. Act XXX, of 1923.
9. of 1933.
10. of 1938.
11. Act No. XXVIII of 1946.
12. cf. Fakirguda V. Cangi, 22, B 227.
13. cf. Mathusami V. Masilamani, 33 M, 342.
14. Bombay Act XXV (of 1946).
15. No. XXII of 1947.
16. Act No. 43 of 1954.
17. The Special Marriage Act, 1954, Pub. by Ram Narain Lal Beni Prasad, Allahabad, 1971. and The Special Marriage Act - 1954 - 9th Oct., Pub. by Delhi Law House, Sec. 24.
18. No. 25.
19. Vide Sec. 5, clause (1).
20. Nehru Papers, 7 May, 1909.
21. *The Discovery of India*, p. 44.
22. Krishna Bhatia, *Indira Gandhi : A Biography of Prime-Minister* (London, 1974, p. 95).
23. *Marriage and Family in India*, by K.M. Kapadia, 1959, p.117.

CHAPTER - IX

Views of Scholars & Writers

Let us discuss the views of some eminent scholars, on the intercaste marriage in India, who may be regarded as intellectual giants in respective spheres and who contributed much to the making of modern India.

Rammohan is the fountain-head of the renaissance of Bengal in the 19th century and hence in all social spheres his social influence was keenly felt. He tried his best to revive the religion of Truth, as pronounced in Vedantic texts on the basis of which the Brāhma-dharma was established. The Brāhma-sabhā on 20.8.1828 may be taken as the starting point of Brāhma movement. His religion may be better called as Universal religion, as Shibnath Sastri[1] would have us believe. Kishorichand Mitra[2] remarks - "What Rammohan wanted was not unity of creed or the creation of a separate religious community like that of the Brāhmas but to introduce monotheistic worship, to establish a universal church where all classes of people, Hindus, Mohammedans and Christians would be all alike welcome to unite in the worship of their supreme and common Father". Debendranath was deeply attracted to Rammohan when in 1838 he came across the first verse of the Īśopaniṣad, edited by Rammohan and he accepted the vow of Brāhmadharma along with 20 associates, swearing before Ramchandra Vidyā-Vāgīsh in 1843. In 1858 Keshab Sen joined the Brāhma movement - when he was fortunate enough to read the article, 'The characteristics of Brāhma-dharma', written by Rajnarayan Bose. In 1865 Keshab Sen differed from Debendranath Tagore on some points of social reform, Keshab Sen, leader of the younger section did away with conservative character of the society and introduced the intercaste marriage and also the widow-remarriage in the society and went even to the length of giving up the sacred thread of the Brāhmaṇa sons.

In 1865 was established also the Brāhma-samāj, under the inspiration of Keshab Sen and women of this society attended openly (and not behind the purdah) the Māghotsava in 1866, to the utter dismay of the older members of Brāhma-samāj. On July 2, 1865 Keshab Sen and his friends wrote to Debendranath with the proposal of some reforms in the working of the society, the first and foremost of which was that the Āchārya of Brāhma-samāj would not henceforth bear any symbol indicating sectarian spirit or caste-distinctions. This clash between two groups ended in the establishment of 'Indian Brāhmasamāj' in 1866, Nov. 11, aiming at religious unity of the whole of India and the mantra *'Suviśālam-idam Viśvaṃ pavitraṃ brahma-mandiram'* - composed with a liberal outlook speaks for the ideal of the younger group led by Keshab Sen.

Keshab Sen also established the 'Bhāratāśrama' and 'Vāmāhitaiṣiṇī-sabhā' on 5 April, 1872 with the mission of thorough reform of women's life in India. Thus the Indian Brāhmasamāj was gradually turned into 'Navavidhāna' on 26 January, 1880 with the idea of incorporating all religions in it and placing it on a higher level, quite aloof from narrow sectarianism and giving scope to the cultivation of the spirit of religious toleration-*sarva-dharma-samanvaya*. It encouraged the extinction of provincialism by means of intercaste or interracial marriage. Keshab Sen established the 'Āryanārī-samāj' in 1879 for the revival of the ideals of Aryan women. Frankly speaking, Keshab Sen wedded spiritual culture with social reform and this 'Nava-vidhān' contributed much towards eradication of castesystem, equalisation of man and woman, spread of female education and liberty of women, development of backward classes and composition of code of intercaste marriage. Thus in the first half of the 19th cent. Hinduism was much influenced by Christianity and Brāhmaism, but in the second half Bankim revived Aryanism, first under the influence of Comte and next of the *Gītā*.

In 1878 (15 May) Sādhāran Brāhma-samāj was founded as a result of internal quarrel in Indian Brāhmasamāj. However, Keshab had to face fiery criticism on the question of marriage of his eldest daughter of thirteen years with the prince of Coochbehar, held on 6.3.1878 and Max Müller[3] says that he did so under 'providential interposition'.

Bankim Chandra,[4] while tracing the history of the Bengalees, speaks of two groups of the non-Aryans—the Dravidians and the Kols, who were gradually Aryanised. He remarks that mixed castes grew up out of mixture, legal or illegitimate union of the Aryans and non-Aryans; and numerous subcastes were developed out of fusion of these mixed castes. He adds that some of the Bengalee śūdras belong to pure Aryan groups but others are mixed products, born of intercaste-marriage or interracial fusion.

The activities of Young Bengal Party, headed by Michael Madhusudan Dutta, show how the young folk of Bengal some of whom were highly enlightened revolted against the rules of the conservative Hinduism and some of them took to evil practices like drinking, some others were baptised and great souls like Madhusudan did not hesitate to embrace Christianity and marry a christian girl. Hence intercaste marriage crept into even the enlightened section of the Hindu community in the 19th cent. A.D.

Ramakrishna appeared as a saint in Bengal with his idea of religious tolearation - *sarva-dharma-samanvaya*, teaching the golden lesson that all religions are but different paths leading to the same goal of Godhood. The Ramakrishna Mission, founded by Vivekananda and other devotees of Ramakrishna is now well-known to the entire globe for its missionary activities for the good of mankind. Vivekananda's idea about intercaste marriage is reflected in a talk with one of the persons who waited upon him at the house of Balaram Bose at 57 Ramkanta Bose Street, Calcutta on 22 and 24 January, 1898. He supported the introduction of the system of intercaste marriage in Indian society at least to avoid physical weakness of the people. Of course, no such matrimonial relationship among heterogenous elements like different religious sects is desireable, because it would lead to loosening the solidarity of the society. He quotes Krishṇa's lesson from the *Gītā* (1.39 *Kulakṣaye praṇaśyanti kuladharmāḥ sanātanāḥ*). He, however, encourages intercaste marriage among the people of the same religion. He advises us to avoid union between a Bengalee and a Madrasee or one of Western India and discloses the secret of going "by the way of least possible resistance". What he wanted to start with is that marriage may be allowed between different communities of Kāyasthas like Uttara-rāḍhī, Dakṣiṇarāḍhī, Vaṅgaja and others. According to him, the system of marriage within a particular class of the same community running for hundreds of years results in physical weakness out of pollution of blood; and that is why infusion of new blood is required for the production of healthy generation at present. But at the same time he insisted on a moral development of the people and building of good character of boys and girls. Elsewhere[5] he criticises the western people as individualistic in character and says that they marry only to satisfy their own individual desires, to the utter neglect of the interests of other people of the society. But he reminds us of the fundamental key to the Indian society. An individual of the Indian society is born and lives only for the interests of the varṇa or caste he belongs to. In this sense the Western people are individualistic from their very birth, while the Indian or at least the Hindu is wholly socialistic. That is why lovemarriage is not encouraged in India, both in ancient and even in modern society. It is interesting to note that Vivekananda was not in favour of widow-remarriage; and he thinks that a woman, if devoted to ideals of Hindu Dharma is generally found to have turned her attention to religious pursuits of life.

It is interesting to note that Rāmakrishṇa's was the spiritual marriage on the soul plane even in this age of senses and he regarded his wife, all along the blessed virgin Sāradādevī as the manifestation of his Divine Mother. His is the living example of the mission of establishing harmony between different religious sects and creeds. This lofty ideal arrested the attention of the thinking section of humanity at large. The current of intercaste marriage gained momentum in the cultured society of the 19th century and the Brāhmasamāj and Āryasamāj, we have already discussed, accelerated the motion of the new movement in the higher section of the community in the eastern and western corners of India. Like Vivekananda, Abhedananda imbibed the spirit of equality and harmony among people of all religions, irrespective of caste or creed. Abhedananda[6] thinks: "We must not consider that non-brahmins are degraded. They are the sons of God, just as much as brahmins are. Pariahs must not be down-trodden and deprived of their privileges........ The soul of a Pariah is as great as the Ātman of the well qualified Brahmin". According to Abhedananda Hinduism should be better called Vedicism or Aryan religion. The Hindus of modern times trace their descent from the great Ṛṣis of the Vedic period and feel proud of their exalted lineage. He thinks that this noble pride has prevented them from intermarrying with foreigners or invading nations. Thus they have tried to save themselves from fusion with external elements and to maintain the Aryan blood pure and unadulterated. Hindu society is divided into numerous communities, each community having several clans and each clan possessing its own peculiar customs. Jāti-dharma means the social laws regulating a particular community. Each Hindu is expected to live in perfect harmony with the customs of the family (Kula), of the clan (gotra) and above all, of the community. Thus he has to curb his desire and live a life of self-sacrifice in the larger interests of the community. The Jāti-dharma is so perfectly organised in India. It is interesting to note that each community is "like a small social republic in itself". Swami Abhedananda[7] says: "The rules and customs of one community do not interfere with those of another, and in this respect every community enjoys absolute freedom as a body but the individuals in it can not enjoy this freedom. They must obey the laws of their community; and if they violate any existing custom, they must go through certain penances and austerities. Otherwise they will be excommunicated". "The social status of a Hindu depends upon the rights which he or she has acquired by birth in the family, clan and community;"[8] and these communities again are subdivisions of larger classes, known in English as castes. The term 'caste' is the Anglicised form of the Portuguese word 'Casta' which means breed or stock. The Sanskrit word which has been translated (or mistranslated) by caste is 'varṇa' (colour) which implied some ethnological distinction of complexion as separating the dominant from the inferior classes - the Aryans from the non-Aryans, aboriginal tribes of ancient India. R.C. Dutta[9] also says, "The very word 'varṇa' which in later Sanskrit indicates caste, is used in the Ṛgveda to distinguish the Aryans and the non-Aryans, and nowhere indicates separate sections in the Aryan community". From the *Gītā* IV.13, also we know that a man's caste was determined not only by his colour but also by his natural qualifications. Obviously when the society required division of labour, they were divided into different classes, according to their natural tendencies. But at first these divisions, specially in the Vedic period, were flexible and interchangeable. That is why, we have so many instances in our sacred literature that the brahmins could intermarry with kṣattriyas, vaiśyas and śūdras. The brāhmaṇas could also be warriors, if they were so qualified and kṣattriyas were sometimes teachers of philosophy, not only in the brahmanical but also in other rival camps like Buddhism and Jainism. Almost all the incarnations of God in India were kṣattriyas. The *Mahābhārata*[10] mentions through Bhṛgu: "There is no distinction of castes. The whole world being created by Brahmā in the beginning consisted of Brahmins only. By actions it underwent the distinctions of caste". Thus the different varṇas lost their flexible nature and turned into rigid hereditary castes as early as the period of the Buddha when the Lord Buddha raised his voice against the priestly power and hereditary caste-divisions. The Buddhists did away with all caste-distinctions and allowed social and political freedom to all. But with the decline of Buddhism the orthodox brahmins reestablished the hereditary caste system. The Muslims came and tried to destroy the social structure of the Hindus but those who were intermarried with the Muslims were excommunicated. But with the advent of the English rule in India and the simultaneous spread of education, the cry for social reform was heard in the 19th cent. A.D., as noted before. The leaders of India tried to unify all communities into one homogenous whole and to make every one feel that he is a member of the Indo-Aryan nation as a whole. The remedy of social evils was discovered by Śrī Rāma Krishṇa in the all-embracing and unifying system of Vedanta which declared the divine right of all humanity, irrespective of caste, creed or colour and taught that all are children of God.

Last of all let us turn our attention to some literary works of the modern period of Indian history, bearing on the social aspect. R.C. Dutt noted the importance of literary evidence as to India's social history: "the literature of every country, slowly expanding through successive ages, reflects accurately the manners and customs, the doings and the thoughts of the people". Ramesh Chandra wrote two social novels 'Saṁsār' in 1886 and 'Samāj' in 1894 in which he pleaded for widow-remarriage and inter-caste marriage. We may quote here the remark of Rameschandra on his two novels: "On principle intercaste marriage is a duty with us because it unites the divided and enfeebled nation, and we should establish this principle (as well as widow-marriage etc.) safely and securely in our little society, so that the greater Hindu society, of which we are only a portion and the advanced guard, may take heart and follow. I can not tell you how deeply I have felt this for years past; of my last two novels, Saṁsar goes in for widow marriage and Samāja.... goes in for intercaste marriage. Bankim had already written social novels. He was not in favour of widow-marriage, as exhibited in the tragic end of Kundanandinī. Though widow-marriage was legalised, it was rarely accepted in the society. He thought that social reform would be done by the propagation of education (and not simply by legistation). Intercaste marriage was neither the topic of legislation, nor of the popular discussion. Rameschandra did his best and was the pioneer of writing on this subject as a leader of social reform movement in those days. He believed that both legislation and literature are equally important to make the society better. Rāmaprasad Saraswatī has been painted as knowledge of religious scriptures incarnate and he aims at social reforms. From the study of character like Śarat and Sudhā it is evidently clear that the writer does not face the problems which arise out of widow remarriage and inter-caste-marriage. 'Bilāsī' was another novel, written in 1920 on intercaste marriage between a Brahmin Mṛtyuñjaya and a Gipsy girl named Bilāsī, belonging to a low caste. Mṛtyuñjaya was attracted to her for her service at his sick bed.

Rabindranath's comment on the system of Hindu marriage deserves our attention: He[11] opines that as the society has been undergoing changes incourse of its evolution, the rules of old society are not always conducive to something good in the new state of the society and hence we should review how far we should obey the laws of the past society at present, specially the regulation of early marriage and also of the system of choice of partners. Elsewhere in an article, Ātmaparicaya[12] the poet has drawn our attention to what the members of the Hindu Society should do: "To practise what is good to all and that is the dharma (duty) of the Hindus". He speaks of the practice of intercaste marriage in the Hindu society from very early times. It is interesting to note that according to Rabindranath the Hindu is the product of evolution of the history of India with its essence of jāti (*Hindu Bhāratvarṣer itihāser ekṭi jātigata pariṇām*). He tried to explain that a society is above its various sects. The Hindu is an all-comprehensive term including different sects like a Brāhma, nay even the votaries of Islam and Christians. Individuals like Kalicharan Banerjee, and Krishna Mohan Banerjee who were converted to christianity were, after all, Hindus embracing the religion of a particular sect. The Brāhma-samāj is, in his opinion, the manifestation of an idea of the Hindu society. Hence we must not forsake any man of our Hindu society and we must practise what is the best virtue of Hindus. Rabindranath has raised his voice against caste-discrimination which breeds hatred towards a section of men, as reflected in the words of Pareshbābu to Sucharitā in his "Gorā".[13] Some of the remarks put in the mouths of different persons in the novel - "Gorā" deserve our closer attention to understand Rabindranath's idea about the Hindu society and also indirectly about the concept of Hindu marriage.

Āandamayī asks Sucaritā whether the Brāhmasamāj would not allow the union of two individuals overcoming the smaller differences of religious sects.[14] Binay[15] says elsewhere that the Hindu samāj has accepted all along new religious sects and hence it is meant for all, irrespective of parties or sects. When Binay expressed his desire to marry Lalitā without the medium of Śālagrāmstone, as desired in Hindu society, Pareshbābu warned him that "marriage is not a mere personal affair but a social institution"[16] and asked him to decide accordingly. Again we find in the letter of Pareshbābu to Binay[17] the more serious advice that if Binay decides to break the rules of Hindu society and marry Lalitā, bred and brought up in a Brāhma family, they must be higher or better then even the society. That means, love, pure and unfliching triumphs above all barriers of caste or creed. Last of all, at the end of the novel Gorā who was so long obstinately fighting for the religious practices of the Hindu society was informed of his identity that he was born of an Irishman and he realised that he was an Indian and he had no conflict with anybody else, a Hindu, a Muslim or a Christian. He was ultimately initiated by Pareshbābu with the Mantra of the Universal God who knows no distinction between religious sects and who is accepted as the presiding Deity of India. Ultimately he was married with Sucharitā with a new idea, revealed to him. Thus this novel teaches us the lesson that marriage is not a personal matter but a social institution and marriage by choice, if sanctified with true love, not simply physical desires but inner desire solemnised on a stronger foundation, must triumph and this was the ideal concept of Hindu marriage of Rabindranath who was above all religious barriers and worshipper of one Lord (*EKO avarṇa*).

In the previous chapter on social reform movement in the 19th cent. A.D. we have discussed different social problems like child-marriage, widow-marriage, female education and interdining of castes and intercaste marriage. The object of social reformers was always to improve the condition of women. Telang worked a miracle in social activities of the Bombay Presidency during the last three decades of the 19th century. All the social reformers of that period received considerable cooperation from the British Law Courts, as evidenced by a High Court judgement delivered by Justice West and Justice Birdhood round about 1886: "Under no circumstances should the Judge force him (a candidate selected by the girl's parental relations) or any other man on the girl whose views were to be consulted before the final selection". Different social evils like Kulīnism, child-marriage, polygamy, widow-burning, drinking habits etc. are reflected in the dramatic literature of Bengal written from the 19th cent. onward. Ramnarayan's Kulīn-kulasarvasva may be cited as an initial attempt to oust kulīnism from the society of Bengal. Madhusūdan, Dīnabandhu and others wrote different plays to eradicate social evils of the day, obviously responding to the call of the society which underwent changes with the introduction of western education and culture into it. Love-marriage was imported into the society of Bengal after the Western fashion as reflected in the play called Līlavatī of Dīnabandhu, written in 1867. Bankimbabu commented in 1877 on the affair of love between Lalita and Līlavatī, painted by Dīnabandhu that this sort of love was a new scene in Bengali society. Such love marriage was also the nucleus of a play 'Māṭirghar' written by Bidhayak Bhattacharya in 1939, where the social life of a city like Calcutta is drawn and which paints unmarried girls as moving freely like western girls and deciding their marriage of their own accord. But we can not deny that though love-marriage takes place in recent days in numerous cases, yet these have not yet been wholeheartedly supported by the society. The society of Bengal, nay of India still looks askance at such incidents, though they are accepted with reluctance as cases of civil marriage. Even in western countries such love-marriage does not bring peace and stability in all cases and hence cases of divorce are increasing in those places. But in Indian society which is more conservative in character and which admits of no divorce under normal circumstances such things are rarely appreciated and sometimes end in miseries. As an instance we may cite 'chārpātra' of Āśāpūrṇā Devī in 1960 which tells us the tale of such divorce of marriage, which is, after all, established by recent legislation of the Government of India. Love-marriage in different circumstances is painted in novels of Bengali literature, specially of Śaratchandra, Tārāśaṅkar and others but it is interesting to note that on intercaste marriage no novel was written in the 19th cent. Intercaste marriage crept into Indian society as nothing but a personal matter. The social reform movement of the 19th cent. aimed at reforms from the larger interests of humanity and at betterment of women's life. Hence intercaste marriages took place, as at present, merely as a personal matter in a particular family, enlightened with ideas of western education; and they received protection from the Government of India after the passing of the Civil Marriage Act, already discussed in detail.

The system of 'a-sagotra' marriage in Hindu society has been discussed, which may be called clan-exogamy or sometimes territorial exogamy; and this system was in practice in many primitive societies of the globe. Paṇḍits are not unanimous on the utility of such system. Some think of the Hindu system of marriage within one's caste but outside one's clan or gotra as an ideal because ancient Indian culture has been preserved in and through this system. The varṇāśramadharma, as practised from the Vedic age has been able to sustain the purity of the society. Restrictions as to union between the white and the black people in South Africa and in America are in practice with the same motive. But some scholars opine in a different tune that marriage exclusively within one's own caste is not conducive to good on the psychological and biological grounds. That is why the girl belonging to the same gotra or same piṇḍa is not allowed to be married. Some scientists of the modern age established with argument that sagotra marriage alone is good for the society and they do not support even 'A-sagotra' marriage, may an intercaste union. They argue that western people have mixed with eastern ones through marriage and we have the rise of Anglo-Indians in India, Anglo-Burmese in Burma and Anglo-Chinese in China; but nowhere we find the rise of great souls like Śaṅkara, Ramakrishṇa, Rabindranath etc. among these mixed people, as remarkably exhibited in the Hindu Society, regulated by traditional rules of marriage. The English are regarded as a great people and many a genius is born in their society. Hence these scholars conclude that a good child is born out of marriage between persons of nearer blood-relationship, i.e., the sagotra marriage is the ideal system, as reflected in a paper read in All India Science Conference at Nagpur by Prof. K.C. Mukherjee of Calcutta University, Dept. of Psychology, and this theory has been tentatively accepted by all scholars of East and West. Hence there is no question of supporting intercaste marriage as it is not appreciated in Hindu scriptures nor by modern scientists who think of marriage as a medium of bringing about a good future of a particular family. Frankly speaking, intercaste marriage is still neglected in Indian society, it is nothing but a personal affair. Though law of the land has accepted it, the society as a whole has not yet come forward to recognise it as a social institution. According to Hindus, children born of such intercaste marriage are not entitled to perform ancestral worship and offer piṇḍa to their manes.

Generally, we find that if any member of a joint family accepts intercaste marriage, he does so independently of other members, by the Civil Marriage Act, sometime beyond the notices of others. However, in some cases where a high-born boy or girl is involved, a social function with the aid of a priest, sometimes in a temple is held even after its registration in a court by the Civil Marriage Act. Enough cases of such marriage are heard of as taking place in Kalighat temple of Calcutta; and sometimes when minor girls are enticed and come to the notice of the Police, their grooms are penalised.

Even in modern India, particularly in Bengal the joint family consists of members of three generations in some cases and at least of two generations. These members, it is quite natural, have difference of opinions and they have always to adjust themselves with others and in cases of intercaste marriage of any member the family peace is lost and in most of the cases the member concerned has to live a separate life and even the parents who have to depend on their only son who has married a girl of a different caste have only to suffer throughout the rest of their life. Hence intercaste marriage is not normally recognised in a society or even in a family. Social plays on this topic have been written in the present century, only a few but none of them have received any larger social recognition.

Widow-remarriage has not been accepted in the Hindu society, though law has approved of it. Similarly the intercaste marriage, though legalised by the special Marriage Act has not been appreciated in the society. However, a few plays written on this topic deserve our attention. Bijan Bhattacharya's "Gotrāntara" paints a picture of such marriage between Gaurī and Kānāi, which is said to have taken place in a refugee colony of the people of East Bengal. Thus this is the instance of intercaste marriage held in distracted conditions of life in refugee camps, far away from the natural environments of social life in Bengal. Another writer, Late Tulasi Lahiri has drawn a picture of such marriage held between a Hindu and a Muslim in 'Bāṅglār Māṭi', which is also equally inspired by the disturbed circumstances of Bengal after its recent partition.The play "Kharā nadīr srote", written by Sunil Datta is a trajedy which paints love between Kāñcana, daughter of a Zeminder and a low-born Sāgar. Another work of Abhijit, known as 'Asavarṇa' shows how the intercaste marriage between Binay Chatterjee and Mālā, daughter of Abinash Datta, both loving each other was not allowed by Binay's guardian at first but accepted in the long run. Thus these few plays show only the complexity growing out of such love marriage between members of different castes, far away from the real solution of the problems, created by personal desires and under economic pressures. Such cases breed only conflicts of mind and complexity of life.

The Hindu Marriage Act has, however, helped a citizen of India to be freely united in marriage with any one, irrespective of caste or creed. Hindu marriage has lost its character as a sacrament, no doubt and the Hindu Marriage Divorce Act has given ample scope to husband or wife for separation of marriage tie. Hindu scripture sanctions re-marriage of women under certain circumstances, as noted in *'naṣṭe mṛte pravrajite klīve ca patite patau pañcasvāptsu nārīṇāṃ pati-r-anyo vidhīyate'*. But in spite of such religious sanction widow-remarriage and divorce-system became obsolete in the Indian society. Now these Acts have ushered in remarkable changes in the society, as evident from the increase of suits filed for divorce every year in Indian courts, by both the sexes, belonging to higher middle-class families. Seniormost pleaders opine that this Act has done more harm than good to the society; whereas younger pleaders think that this Act is good for the society, specially for the women who were so long suffering from their husband's torture. There is no doubt that this Act has eaten into the vital force of Hindu marriage which had too long been accepted, as a sacrament and an indissoluble tie. But the Hindu society as a whole has raised no protest against this Act and no social movement was started against it. Inter-caste marriage and divorce of marriage — these are still personal affairs and are but stray cases in the society. Not a single woman, even winning decree of divorce has been able to get herself rehabilitated in the society after being married again. In most cases of intercaste marriages where physical attraction and not pure love unites two souls, the two get separated by taking advantage of this Act of divorce.Two Bengali plays, 'Dāvi' by Devanarayan Gupta and 'Śreyasī' by Subodh Ghosh may be referred to, as showing the denoument of such marriages.

Life at present in India as elsewhere is mainly influenced by new forces working behind the city-life as a result of industrialisation and urbanisation. Even a peaceful life at villages is disturbed by such forces which create new problems. Village life is generally more peaceful, as its essence is more or less moral and hence economic hardship is tolerated for the realisation of a higher moral ideal. But city-life is more or less based on individualism and so an individual craves for satisfying his personal interests at the cost of higher social ideals. Economic development of our land has brought about substantial changes in our life, and now-a-days there is little difference between rural and urban areas, both being moulded by new norms of industrial life. Industrialisation has placed before all people of the world one and the same goal of life, viewed from economic standpoint. In India, particularly in Bengal we meet tussle between two forces, forces of industrial culture of city-life and under-current forces of old traditions and ageworn customs of the land. Spread of women's education, liberty to both sexes to mix together freely in schools, colleges and offices and after all, new Acts of marriage, discussed before have encouraged young folk to marry and collect their partners, according to their own choice and some cases where social forces create hindrance at such unions, end in tragedy. Of course, souls are not wanting even in city-life, who pursue their moral ideals. But life, based upon mere moral ideals fails to keep pace with real life, full of stern complexities and hence it may satisfy our academic curiosity alone. True indeed, economic life has and is going to determine the social life of the people all over the globe, and even in India. Instead of dharma which once regulated the life of the people, nationalism is ruling the inner spirit of our life and even in India, people think in terms of the country or nation as a whole and they are trying their best to improve their economic lot. Hence it is quite natural for the enlightened section of India to turn their attention to build one and undivided life, where there should be no barriers of caste or creed and where India would flourish with international life and culture, as reflected in the ideal of Viśva-Bhāratī, founded by Rabindranath Tagore, expressed in '*yatra viśvaṃ bhavatyeka-nīḍam*'.

But Sridhar Venkates Ketkar, an eminent Maraṭhi writer and historian (b. 1884 d. 1937) has drawn our attention to some problems arising out of intercaste marriage in his Maraṭhi novel "Brāhmaṇ-Kanyā". Śāntābāī, mother of Kālindī was married with a Brahmin pleader named Āppā Saheb; and Ketkar comments on such intercaste marriage: "The reformists, seated on an easychair began to talk after the marriage of Śāntābāī that it brought a social problem of caste-distinction to a happy end. Yet as a matter of fact the problem was not solved, rather it started anew". Āppā Saheb, being a brahmin was always conscious of his birth in a higher family and he thought that his children, brought up in a brahmanical tradition of life would be recognised in the society. But the future life of Kālindī and other children, as painted shows how they had to face stern realities of life in the society, far away from what may be called social recognition. Hence such intercaste marriage creates various problems for the next generation, no doubt but in the present economic conditions of life in the society as a result of urbanisation and industrialisation, new ideas of political and social life are strong enough to revolutionise our standard and cleavage between conservative elements and liberal section, more enlightened would, it may be hoped, bring an era of unrest in the social life of India in the interim period and time would alone show how far radical changes would be adjusted to needs of the modern society, to the establishment of peace and harmony in the life of heterogenous diverse elements of India.

REFERENCES

1. *History of Brāhmasamāj*, p. 51.
2. *Calcutta Review*, No. LXXXVII, p. 232.
3. *Biographical Essays* (of Maxmüller) p. 114.
4. *Bankim-Rachanāvalī* (Bengali) Sāhitya-Saṃsad, p. 344 ff.
5. Vivekananda *Vāṇī O Rachanāvalī*, Vol. V, pp. 434-439.
6. *Complete works of Swami Abhedananda*, (Ramakrishna Vedanta Math, Calcutta, 1967), Vol. VII, p. 545.
7. *Ibid.*, Vol. II, p.56.
8. *Ibid.*, pp. 58-59.
9. *Civilisation in Ancient India*, Vol. I, p. 65.
10. Śānti-parvan, ch. 188-189.
11. 'Samāj' in Rabindra-*Rachanāvalī*, 13th Kāṇḍa, pp. 72-101
12. Parichaya' - Rabindra-Rachanāvalī, 13th Kāṇḍa, pp. 165-179.
13. *R.R.* Kāṇḍa 9, p. 116.
14. *Ibid.*, p. 230.
15. *Ibid.*, p. 272.
16. *Ibid.*, p. 274.
17. *Ibid.*, p. 283.

APPENDIX
Rabindranath on Marriage

Let me conclude this treatise with the view of Rabindranath in greater detail about the system of marriage in India and also on the intercaste marriage among the Hindus. Rabindranath thinks that marriage is like all other matters of a civilised society nothing but the attempt to establish a treaty between the intention of nature and that of man. Society runs under the rule of dichotomy of two natures of a living being and of nature of society. The Aryans in India were first dwellers in forest before they settled in villages and towns. Cows were their first wealth and cattle-rearing became their livelihood. The importance of cattle-rearing was superceded by that of agriculture on plains of river-valleys. Capture and stealing of cattle were the main cause of fighting in the Vedic age, whereas stealing of Sītā (agricultural land) became the main factor of epic struggle as in the *Rāmāyaṇa*. The history of India in the age of the *Rāmāyaṇa* draws our eyes to three factors like the Aryans, the monkeys and the Rākṣasas. Ultimately the Kṣattriya kings paid more attention to peace than to struggle in social life. Heroism in the sphere of peace-policy required renunciation or resignation, as reflected in the Rāmāyaṇa which sings of the glory of domestic life by the maintenance of peaceful existence in the family consisting of father, mother, brothers, sons, husbands and wives, a king and his subjects and masters and servants. It insists also on the preservation of truth of pledges, as in case of Daśaratha to Kaikeyī. Household-life is the most essential element of Hindu society and hence marriage is the most important factor, established even in the Dharmaśāstras: "*Gṛhastha eva yajate gṛhastha-s-tapyate tapah/ caturṇām-āśramānāṃ tu gṛhastha-s-tu viśiṣyate//.*"

The essence of social life in India lies in the joint effort of the members of the society in observing the duties of the life of a householder, the most important of which is the curbing of the desires of individuals for the good of the society as a whole. Marriage is at the root of a householder's life and it is regulated by so many rules. The forms of marriage like gāndharva, rākṣasa, āsura and paiśāca were accepted even by Manu as valid in the society, though there are the manifestations of individual desires and not at all of social ones. But these forms were, however, denounced, though accepted. The Kṣattriyas who intended to conquer and rule could not be curbed by the society, I mean, by the joint effort of a big social organisation. We must remember that revolution in society or religion was made in ancient India by Kṣattriyas like Buddha, Mahāvīra and Kṛṣṇa. Manu defines 'gāndharva' as the system of marriage, born of the mutual consent of a bride and her groom. That means, it was looked askance at as being born of desires (Kāma). Definitely it cared little for social good and more for the satisfaction of individual desires.

Rabindranath raised the question of eugenics of the people of western civilisation. Science cares little for individual emotions and the path of individual desires should be avoided if we intend to create desireable children. Marriage should be restricted in cases of diseases like leprosy or mental disorder of persons concerned. Our society is more concerned with rites and practices of a particular sect and so the principles of marriage were formulated accordingly. Kālidāsa paints the picture of gāndharva marriage in Abhijñāna-śakuntalam and Kumārasambhavam, nay even in Raghuvaṃśam; and he speaks of marriage as penance and not at all the means of satisfaction of physical desires. Marriage was meant for curbing desires and producing a good son (Kumāra). However, this curbing does not mean that there was no scope for love in conjugal life. In India at least the conjugal relation between husband and wife was cemented by some sort of idea behind the question of love. The wife submitted or still submits herself to her husband as an embodiment of idea, an ideal love. The influence of a woman upon the mind of her husband is known as śakti (power) in India; really this is sweatness in their conjugal life. Woman is of two types; one is the aspect of mother by which she creates and rears her children as good, another is the charming aspect (preyasī), noted as śakti or 'mādhurya'. Śaṅkara has described this sweeter aspect of śakti in Ānandalaharī. This sweeter power of woman is best expressed when human civilisation reaches the stage of spiritual level. But this standard of spiritual excellence in our life has not yet been reached and that is why man and wife are not in the same level. Man still looks upon his wife as good as gold (Kāñcana); he may accept or reject her at his sweet will.

Rabindranath speaks of the Hindus as a nation (jāti), formed as a whole consisting of different elements from the Vedic age onward upto the epic period, unified by injunctions of scriptures, sacraments, rules and customs and also by the gradual absorption of various peoples from the Dravidians in the south to the Nepalese on the north. The difference between the Aryans and non-Aryans in colour, customs and physical features is lost and they have formed as a result of intermixture of blood and culture a comprehensive body, known as Hindu. We have already traced the history of intercaste marriage between Aryans and non-Aryans, the śūdras, known as pratiloma since the early Vedic period and specially during the period of the rise of Buddhism. In the later period the society, reformed by new rules and regulations became unified as a whole, known as Hindu society. In the subsequent period the Muslims and English came to India and added something new to the ancient culture of the Hindus. We have also traced the history of reform movement of the Hindus in the nineteenth century A.D. and we must always remember the contributions of many a genius like Rammohan Roy, Bankim, Ranade, Vivekānanda and others, which enriched the old culture with new treasures and built the new society with modern Indian civilisation. The Viśva-Bhāratī as an institution is meant for the fuller understanding of the culture of the East and the West, where the whole world would meet together and build a new culture.

About the age of marriage Rabindranath thinks that considering the social benefits we should change the rules of earlier jurits and it is better to follow scientific reasons for the procreation of healthy children. He reminds us of the view of Dr. Mahendra Lal Sarkar that early marriage should be avoided, because a male and a female are not fit for producing children as soon as they reach the first stage of youth. Some accept the age between 24 and 30 for the male and the age between 8 and 12 for the female. Candranathbabu opines that a male should be of mature age, considering the fact that the wife must be fully identified with her husband. Some plead for the early age of the wife so that she may serve the joint-family of the Hindus. Some scholars try to show purity and spiritualism of Hindu marriage with quotations from ancient scriptures. But our society at present differs from that of Manu and others. The days of Manu with old system of education, brahmacarya, upanayana, life in the house of a 'guru' etc. are gone and at present we do not follow the rules of Manu and others. Rabindranath refers to Candranath Bose and his comment on Hindu wife and Hindu marriage, well appreciated by Akṣaya Kumar Sarkar. Candranathbabu speaks of Hindu wives not only as equal to their husbands but also as their deities: "*Yatra nārya-s-tu pūjyante ramante tatra devatāḥ*", i.e., gods are pleased where women are worshipped. But Rabindranath differs from him and refers to some demerits of Hindu women shown in Manu. We know that Comte speaks of religious attitude and qualities of head and heart of a wife, far superior to those of a husband and he asserts emphatically that the moral and spiritual life of a male can not be made perfect without the help of his female partner. Manu did not follow what we come across in Comte. Bhīṣma and Yudhiṣṭhira of the *Mahābhārata* also mention the demerits of women. Chandranathbabu speaks highly of the position of married women in Hindu society as good as that of a goddess. But it is well known to us that the husband is a god to his wife in Hindu society but not the *vice versa*. We can not forget the scene of Draupadī being insulted by Kīcaka before her husbands. Even most respected elders did not move to protect her prestige. The idea of complete identification between husband and wife is regarded as the ideal of Hindu marriage; but this can not be taken to be proved at least in cases of polygamy and of kulinism. Besides, Hindu marriage is a sacrament and not a contract, at least according to Dharma school. But the divorce system was allowed in the society in the eye of the Artha-school and so the principle of identification between the two is out of question.

Rabindranath looks upon the Brāhmasamāj as the natural expression of the history of Hindu society. (Cf. Paricaya, *Rabindra-racanāvali*, vol. 13, p. 172). The duty of the Hindu society is to observe or practise what is 'dharma', i.e. to do good to the members of the society. The question here is the caste-distinction and if we believe this casteism as bad, we can not claim to be Hindu, being the supporter of this evil practice. In that case as a Hindu we must fight against it even while living in the midst of Hindus. We shall never step back from getting our children married even outside the caste. Thus as a matter of fact this intercaste marriage is the highest ideal of Hindu marriage. It is not a fact that the Hindu society did never allow intercaste marriage and so the present society should not be denounced simply for the approval of such practices. Some may raise a question that if casteism is not accepted,then with whom shall we live in the society? The answer is obviously with those who do not accept caste-distinction and who would gradually form a particular sect. Thus a sect rises from within the society, as for example, a brāhma-sect rises from within the Hindu society. The term 'Hindu' is taken in a broader sense when Rabindranath thinks of some eminent Bengalee Christians like Kali Banerjee, Krishna Mohan Banerjee, Jnanendra Mohan Tagore, as belonging to Christian community within the Hindu caste. He means to say that 'jāti' is superior to one's 'belief' (mata). The baptised christian of the Hindu society is obviously nourished by Hindu ideas even when he changes his religious faith. His spirit of Hinduism lies deeper than that of religious faith like Christianity which he has adopted as a matter of personal belief. The religious truth of Hinduism is universalism which the Hindus have accepted with all their heart and mind. Even in the mode of worship of the

Brāhma-s lies in a deeper layer the truth of Hinduism, revealed in and through the philosophy and the system of devotion (bhakti) and meditation (dhyāna) or the process of Yoga, complete unification of an individual self with the highest self (Brahman).

The earliest stage of the history of India shows the furious struggle between the Aryans and non-aryans. The sacrifice of snakes of Janamejaya indicates the fury of such class-struggle when Janamejaya tried his best to put an end to the non-aryans who were worshippers of snakes. Not the struggle but the peaceful unification of these two races was rendered possible by three Kṣattriyas, Janaka, Viśvāmitra and Rāmachandra, as reflected in the Rāmāyaṇa. Viśvāmitra was the guide of Rāma and he won the truth from Janaka. The brāhmaṇas or kṣattriyas were not of the same path of action, the brahmins were occupied with sacrifices, a life of priests and the kṣattriyas were always engaged in fighting and conquering new territories; and it is they who realised the truth of unity in the midst of diversity, i.e., Brahma-Vidyā. Bhṛgu was the ideal of sacrificers or brāhmaṇas and he struck at the bosom of Viṣṇu, showing the conflict between brāhmaṇism and Vaiṣṇavism. Kṛṣṇa was the teacher of Vaiṣṇavism. Rāma and Kṛṣṇa were the fountain heads of Vaiṣṇavism. Janaka shows the example of the unification of the highest knowledge, bhakti and karman. He made use of 'Brahma-jñāna' and at the same time of art of agriculture by ploughing land.

We can not forget that Rāmachandra was the friend of Guhaka, a Caṇḍāla, deity of the monkeys like Hanumān and friend of Vibhīṣaṇa. Practically he built a bridge of love and good-will between the Aryans and non-aryans. Once the brahmins and kṣattriyas exercised the power of preservation and expansion of self respectively. The Kṣattriyas were bent on expanding or extending their rule or influence in new areas of south India, but the brahmins tried to check them. However, the brahmins linked themselves with fresh peoples obviously the non-aryan by a silken tie of love and goodwill. The history of Rāmacandra shows the forces of love which made monkeys and rākṣasas as his own.

The intermixture of Aryans with non-aryans worked within the society to bring about a cultural union even in the sphere of religion. Śiva was the god of non-aryans and feud between the two went on for a long period of time. Arjuna had once to submit to Śiva, god of the Kirātas. Aniruddha, grandson of Kṛṣṇa stole away Uṣā, daughter of Vānāsura; and Kṛṣṇa won the game. Śiva was not accepted in Vedic sacrifices as a god and so his worshippers destroyed such sacrifices, ultimately Śiva was identifed with Vedic Rudra. Manu's effort to stand against intermixture of blood or Varṇas and condemnation of Devala-brahmins who were engaged in idol-worship shows how the society exerted its best to stand against, though it had to accept such intermixture. There is little doubt that teachers like Buddha and Mahāvīra checked the rising influence of the brahmins for a long period. But after the flood of Buddhism subsided, the unity of the society was broken to a considerable degree owing to intermixture not only with internal non-aryans but also with external ones like Śakas, Hūnas and others. Rabindranath speaks highly of the *Mahābhārata*, specially of the *Gītā* as the manifestation of the inner truth of the Aryan society, the highest essence of Indian history in the shape of assimilation of jñāna, karma and bhakti and also of different systems of Indian philosophy. He refers also to Brahma-sūtra as throwing immense light on the Āryadharma, where Truth has been analysed from the standpoint of dualism and non-dualism. He regards it as the 'dharma' of all humanity.

Rabindranath does never minimise the importance of non-aryans. As a matter of fact the Dravidians of the South India were not inferior to Aryans and their contributions in the expression of sentiments and creative faculty in the field of fine arts (kalā) added something new to the Aryan culture and this composite culture itself is Hindu. Śiva (= Rudra of the Ṛg-veda) represents the yogin enjoying joy of freedom from all desires and the naked ascetic with the spirit of renunciation and he also exhibits the culture of the non-aryans with the concept of ghosts, pretas and persons moving in the burning ground and with their modes of worshipping snakes, bulls, trees and 'liṅga'-s. The Vaiṣṇavism also rises in the unified shape of the Ganges and the Yamunā, preaching detailed description of Kṛṣṇa, as reflected in the *Gītā* and also in tales of Ābhiras, non-aryan cowherds telling their tales of love, beauty and youthful freshness. The union of the Aryans and the Dravidians brought about a wonderful assimilation of Truth (satya) and various forms of beauty (rūpa) in Hindu civilisation. Even in *Devī-tantra* we come across two aspects — Aryan in Haimavatī Uṣā and non-aryan in the terrible shape of Kālī.

In the earliest stage of Indian history we come across a strong conflict between the Aryans and non-Aryans, they were fighting one another but even in the midst of struggle they did not hate one another. The Kṣattriyas, even while fighting with the non-Aryans, united themselves with their enemies, as established by a long list of marriage-alliances between them. Later on when the Rajputs entered into India, the brahmins accepted them like other non-Aryans in the Hindu society and thus we find the rise of an artificial Kṣattriya caste, whose cooperation helped the stability of the brahmanical society. In the medieval period the Hindu society, even in the period of self-contraction exerted for self-expansion to no mean degree as illustrated by the guru-s like Nānak and Kabīr and others. Kabir realised the inner spiritual wealth as the Truth lying in the pit of debris and they wanted to propagate that Truth after doing away with all social customs and scriptural injunctions. The same process of sādhanā in Hindu society is still today running in right earnest. Rabindranath realised the importance of one in many in the eternal sādhanā of India and hence the gravity of marriage-system, particularly intercaste and inter-racial marriage should be well appreciated as a stepping stone to build our nation on a stronger foundation of mutual love and goodwill among different elements of the society.

Bibliography
With Abbreviations

Abbe Dubois, *Character, Manners and Customs of the People of India*

Abhedananda, *Complete works* (Vedanta Math, Calcutta).

A.C. Das, *Ṛgvedic Culture*

Aitareya Brāhmaṇa (A B).

All India Oriental Conference (AIOC)

Annals and Antiquities of Rajasthan (Tod)

Annals of Bhandarkar Oriental Research Institute, Poona

Aparārka

Āpastamba Dharma sūtra (and *śāstra*) (Āpas. D.S.)

Arthaśāstra of Kauṭilya (A Ś).

Āśāpurṇā Devī

(Assam) *District Gazetteer of Lakhimpur*

Atharva-Veda (A.V.)

Ātpur Inscription

Aufrecht-*Ṛgveda*

Baden Powell H.B. - *Indian Village Community*

B.C. Allen - *Assam District Gazetteer*

Ballālasena

Bañkimchandra, *Rachanāvalī*

Bālaṃbhaṭṭa

Bhaṭṭa Bhavadeva - *Prāyaścitta-prakaraṇa* (ed. by G.C. Vidyaratna)

Bhandarkar's List of Inscriptions of North India

Bhattacharya Bijan, *Gotrāntara*

Bhāsa

Bodhāyana Dharmasūtra (Bodh. D.S.)

Bogardus, *Sociology*

Bombay Act - XXV of 1946

Bombay Indian Law Reports

Bṛhaspati-Dharma-sūtra

Bṛhad-devatā

Bṛhatsaṃhitā

Brifault, *Mothers*

Calcutta Indian Law Reports (C.I.L.R.)

Calcutta Review

The Classical Age (Bharatiya Vidyabhavan), Bombay.

D.R. Bhandarkar - *Foreign Elements in the Hindu Population.*

———— *Some aspects of Ancient Indian Culture.*

D.C. Sircar - *Society and Administration of India* (Soc. Ad. In.).

———— *Successors of Sātavāhanas* (Succ. Sāt.) *in Lower Deccan.*

———— *Select Inscriptions* (S.I.)

Daṇḍin - *Daśakumāracaritam* (D K C)

———— *Avantīsundarīkathā* (A S K)

———— *Kāvyādarśa*

D.N. Majumdar, *Races and Cultures of India*

Dīnabandhu Mitra - His works

Discovery of India by J. Nehru

Divyāvadāna

Encyclopaedia of Religion and Ethics (E.R.E.)

Early Brāhmī Records in India, H.P.Chakraborti

F.C. Bailay, *Contributions to Indian Sociology*

Gautama Dharmasūtra (Gaut. D.S.)

Ghurye, G.S, *Caste, Class and Occupation*

Gītā

Gṛhastha - ratnākara

Grierson, *Linguistic Survey of India*

H.C. Roychoudhuri, *Studies in Indian Antiquities, Political History of Ancient India.*

Hemchandra, *Dvyāśraya - mahākāvya*

Harivaṃśa

Harṣacaritam

H.C. Chakladar, *Social Life in Ancient India on Vātsyāyana's Kāmasūtra.*

Hindu Marriage Act, 1955, J.K. Nag, Law Book Stall, Calcutta, 1956.

Hindu Code

Hiraṇyakeśin Gṛhyasūtra

Indian Antiquary (I.A.)

Indo - Asian Culture

Jātakas (Jāt. or J.)

Jīmutavāhana (Dāyabhāga).

Jolly, *Hindu Law and Custom*

Journal of Royal Asiatic Society (J.R.A.S.)

Junagarh ins.

J.N. Banerjee Volume (pub. by Alumini Association), Dept. of A.I.H. & C. - C.U., 1960.

Kālidāsa - *Raghuvaṁśa, Mālavikāgnimitra & Abhijñāna Śakuntalam*

K.P. Jayaswal, *Hindu Polity*

Kāmasūtra

Kapadia K.M., *Marriage and Family in India*

Kathāsaritsāgara (by Somadeva)

Kauṭilya, *Arthaśāstra*

Kauṣītaki Brāhmaṇa (Kauṣ. Brāh).

Keshab Sen

K.C. Mukherjee's paper in A.I. Science Conference, Nagpur

K.S. Sambasivan (Indian Journal of Social Work), 1946-47, Vol. II.

Kirātajanakṛti -

Krishna Bhatiya, *Indira Gandhi*

Krishnanath Chatterjee, *Hindu Marriage in India, Past and Present.*

Kullūka, *Com. on Manu*

Lahiri Tulasi

Lāṭyāyana Śrautasūtra

Lüder's Inscriptions (Lüd. No.)

Mahābhārata (Mbh.)

Mahāvaṃśa

Manusaṃhitā (Manu)

Mānava - Gṛhyasūtra

Mandalik's Hindu Law

MC - Lenan, *Studies in Ancient History*

M.C. Parekh, *The Brāhmasamāj*

Marriage of Cousins in India, W.H.R. Rivers (in JRAS, 1907).

Medhātithi, Com. on Manu

Mīmāṁsā - Sūtra of Jaimini

Mitākṣarā of Vijñāneśvara on *Yājñavalkya-Smṛti*

Muir, *Original Sanskrit Texts*

M.V. Shah, *Social Philosophy of Gandhiji*

Nāgārjunkoṇḍa Pillar ins.

Nehru Papers

Nīlakaṇṭa - Com. on Mbh.

Nirṇayasindhu

Nirukta

N.K. Bose, *Cultural Anthropology*

Origin of Civilisation and Primitive Condition of Man

Parāśara - *Mādhava*

Pāṇini - *Aṣṭādhyāyī*

Pāraskara - *Gṛhyasūtra*

P.V. Kane, *History of Dharmaśāstras* (H.D.Ś) - BORI, Poona

Paiṭhīnasi saṁhitā

Purāṇas - *Vāyū, Viṣṇu, Bṛhad - dharma-purāṇa* and *Brahma-Vaivarta*

Rabindraracanāvalī

R.C. Dutt, *Civilisation in Ancient India*

R.C. Majumdar, *History of Ancient Bengal*

Ṛgveda (ṚV)

R. Shaffer's *Ethnography of Ancient India*

Rājataraṅginī

Rāmacaritam of Sandhyākara Nandī

Rāmāyaṇa

Ray H.C., *Dynastic History of Northern India*, 2 vols, Calcutta, 1931, 1936 (DHNI).

R.B. Pandey, *Hindu Saṃskāras*

R.P. Chanda, *The Indo - Aryan Races*

Risley, *People of India*

Romila Thappar, *Ancient Indian Social History*

Saṇgama Literature

S.V. Ketkar, *Brāhmaṇ - Kanyā*.

Sachau, E.C., *Alberuni's Report*

Sacred Books of the East (SBE) - ed. by Maxmüller, tr. J. Eggling

Śaṁkha saṃhitā

Sarat Chandra Chattopadhyaya, His novels

Śatapatha Brāhmaṇa (Ś B)

Śāntamūla

Senart, *Caste in India*

Sherring, *Hindu Tribes and Castes*

S.K. Chatterjee, *Indo - Asian Culture*

Slater, *Dravidian Elements in Indian Culture*.

Smṛti - Candrikā

Social Reform in Bengal, Sitanath Tattvabhusan

Source material for a history of the Freedom Movement in India (Govt. of Bombay).

Special Marriage Act, 1954 (Act No.43) - Pub. Delhi Law House, 1954.

Sudhakar Chattopadhyaya, *Social Life in Ancient India.*

———— *Traditional values in Indian Life.*

Taittiriya Brāhmaṇa (TB).

Taittiriya Saṁhitā - (TS).

Tarn, *The Greeks in Bactria and India*

T. Watters on Yuan chwang's *Travels in India*

Tippera C.P. ins.

Uśanas (Smṛti).

Vaidya, *Hitaiṣiṇī*

Vasiṣṭha Dharmasūtra (Vas. D.S.)

Vājasaneya Saṃhitā (VS)

V.M. Apte, *The Vedic Age*

The Vedic Age, Majumdar and Altekar

Vijñāneśvara, com. of Mitākṣarā (Vijñā. Mitā.)

Viṣṇu - Purāṇa,

Viṣṇudharmasūtra

Vivekananda's '*Speeches and writings*'

Vivekānanda, *Vāṇi-O-Rachanāvalī.*

Vyāsa (Smṛti).

Westermark, *History of Human Marriage*

Winternitz, *History of Indian Literature* - Eng. tran, C.U. 1927

Yājñavalkya - (Yāj.). with com. of Vijñāneśvara.

INDEX